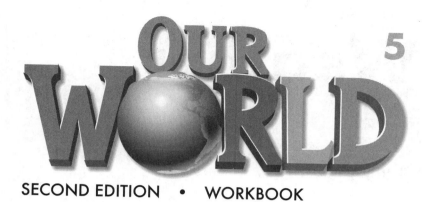

Series Editors
Joan Kang Shin
JoAnn (Jodi) Crandall

T0308273

SECOND EDITION • WORKBOOK

NATIONAL GEOGRAPHIC
L E A R N I N G

Australia • Brazil • Mexico • Singapore • United Kingdom • United States

Unit 1

Extreme Weather

VOCABULARY 1

1 **Read and write.** Do the extreme puzzle!

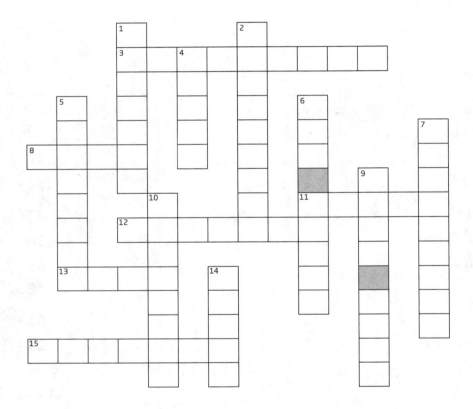

Across

3. Bad storm with very fast, dangerous winds
8. Go up
11. How fast something travels
12. Too little rain
13. Go down
15. Storm with strong, twisting winds

Down

1. Loud noise from a storm
2. Can make night look like day
4. From low to high or high to low
5. Snow falling hard
6. A rainstorm can change into this when it is very cold (two words)
7. Strong winds blowing in a desert
9. Hot for many days (two words)
10. A storm with heavy rain and fast winds
14. Too much water

2 Listen and circle. Listen for the puzzle words. Circle them on the puzzle in Activity 1. TR: 1.1

3 Unscramble the words.

1. egnar _____

2. orpd _____

3. ughdrot _____

4. natdoor _____

5. dazilbrz _____

6. tansmords _____

4 Read and write. Use the words from Activity 3 to complete the sentences.

1. The water in the lake was low because of the _____.

2. The winds from the _____ lifted a car and moved it 30 meters (98 feet)!

3. If there is a _____ in the temperature, I will need to wear a coat.

4. When it is windy in a desert, there can be a _____.

5. What was the _____ of temperatures today, from lowest to highest?

6. In a really bad _____, sometimes all you can see is white!

SONG

1 **Listen and write.** Use verses from the song. **TR: 1.2**

There's bad weather on the way!
There's bad weather on the way!

Is it going to storm? Yes, it is!
Is there going to be lightning? Yes, there is!
Is there going to be thunder? Yes, there is!

When there's going to be a storm,
I hurry inside!

Be prepared for emergencies.
It's always good to be safe. You'll see!
Grab supplies and a flashlight, too.
Seek shelter. It's the safe thing to do!

Is it going to storm? _____ _____

Yes, it is! _____ _____

_____ _____ _____

_____ _____

_____ _____

_____ _____

2 **Write a new verse for the song.**

Is/Are _____? Yes, _____!

Is/Are _____? Yes, _____!

Is/Are _____? Oh, yes _____!

GRAMMAR 1

Future predictions and plans with *be going to*

It's		snow	tomorrow.	It's = It is
I'm	**going to**	stay	home with my mom.	I'm = I am
We're		watch	a movie.	We're = We are

Question						Answer	
	Is	it	**going to**	snow	tomorrow?	Yes, it is. No, it isn't.	
What	**are**	you		do		**I'm going to** stay home.	

Use *be going to* to talk about the future.

1 **Write.** What are they going to do on a rainy Saturday?

1. Mario / walk / in the rain Mario's going to walk in the rain.

2. Pedro / read / newspaper _____

3. I / write / story _____

4. Marta and Carla / listen / radio _____

5. Pablo / sleep _____

2 **Write.** Answer the questions using the given word.

1. What's the weather going to be like tomorrow? (ice storm)
   Tomorrow there's going to be an ice storm.

2. What's going to happen if it rains for another day? (flood)
   _____

3. What are you going to do when there is a drought? (water)
   _____

4. When she sees lightning, what is she going to hear soon after? (thunder)
   _____

5. It's going to snow. What is he going to do? (boots)
   _____

VOCABULARY 2

1 **Read and check.**

What is it?	a plan	a shelter	an emergency
1. A hurricane arrives, and the streets are flooding.			
2. The winds are strong, and trees are falling.			
3. Get fresh water and other supplies.			
4. A room under a house. You can go there during a hurricane.			
5. Have a radio nearby at all times.			

2 **Complete the sentences.** Use words from the box. Some words may be used more than once.

emergency   evacuate   flashlight   plan   shelter   supplies

1. I'm going to take this ___*flashlight*___ with me to a(n) ___*shelter*___.

2. You need a(n) _____ so that you know when to _____.

3. In a(n) _____, you will need _____ like food and water.

4. This is a(n) _____, and everyone must _____ to a(n) _____.

5. My _____ is to keep a(n) _____ with my _____.

GRAMMAR 2

1 **Write what you see.**

1. If she sees a stop sign, <u>she stops her bike.</u>
_____

2. If he sees that it is raining, _____
_____

3. _____
_____ we stand at the bus stop.

4. _____
_____
_____

5. _____
_____
_____

6. _____
_____
_____

7

1 **Listen and read**. TR: 1.3

Weather Change

We've always had extreme weather. Do you know that there is more extreme weather now than in the past? According to many scientists, this change started when people started to burn coal, oil, and gas.

The average temperature on Earth is rising. Some droughts are longer and hotter. More of the ice on mountains melts faster. If this water goes to the sea, the sea level rises.

Different places have different changes in the weather. Some places have less rain. Other places have more rain and floods. In most places, there are more storms. Storms are stronger, too. The warmer sea temperatures make hurricanes stronger.

Weather change is a fact. But we can do something. For example, we can make factories and cars more efficient. That way, we can burn less coal, oil, and gas. We can also build stronger houses in safer areas. We can use less energy.

There are also some practical things that everyone can do to be prepared for more extreme weather. People should have a plan and supplies for emergencies. People who live in areas that can flood or in hurricane areas should evacuate in an emergency.

The coldest temperature ever recorded on Earth was −97.7°C (−144°F) on an ice sheet deep in the middle of Antarctica.

2 Circle the best answer.

1. When the weather gets warmer,

   a. ice on mountains melts faster.

   b. the seas rise.

   c. both a and b.

2. To slow weather change, we can

   a. build stronger houses.

   b. burn less coal, oil, and gas.

   c. both a and b.

3. Hurricanes are stronger because

   a. the sea water is warmer.

   b. droughts are longer and hotter.

   c. people don't evacuate.

3 Write what you learned from the text. Then work with a partner. Compare your answers.

What did you know?

What did you learn?

What do you want to know?

WRITING

1 **Read *Safe not Sorry!* in your Student's Book.** How did the writer plan her writing? Read the steps.

1. The writer chose something that happened.

2. Next, the writer wrote things that happened in the order they happened.

3. Then the writer wrote about her feelings about the things that happened.

Feelings
It was scary, but a little exciting, too.
Everyone was worried.
I am so happy we had a family plan.

4. Next, the writer added descriptions of how she lived the experience through her senses. In the chart below, see the sense words used. Notice that the writer didn't write about all her senses. You can write about all or only some senses.

See	Hear	Touch	Taste	Smell
part of a tree wood on the window	weather forecaster strong winds hard rain loud crash	heavy wood		

5. Next, the writer wrote a first sentence to say what the narrative was about. *If a hurricane comes, we know what to do.*

6. Then the writer wrote what happened in order. She included information about what she saw, what she heard, and how she felt.

7. Finally, the writer wrote a sentence to close the narrative. *Hopefully there isn't going to be a hurricane for a while.*

2 **Plan to write about your extreme weather experience.**
Answer the questions and complete the chart.

1. What extreme weather experience will you write about?

_____

2. What feelings will you write about?

_____

See	Hear	Touch	Taste	Smell

3 **Follow the steps in Activity 1.** In your notebook, write your narrative about an extreme weather experience.

4 **Express yourself.** Plan to write about something that happened to you. Choose one of the items below. Then complete the table.

◯ a happy thing   ◯ a scary thing   ◯ a beautiful thing

What experience will you describe?	What words will you use to describe your senses?	What words will you use to describe your feelings?

5 **Write each thing that happened.** Put the events in order.

1. _____

2. _____

3. _____

6 **Write your personal narrative in your notebook.**

UNIT 1 REVIEW

1 **Read and match.**

1. very, very cold   a. drought

2. winds that spin   b. thunder

3. very hot for a long time   c. ice storm

4. hot, dry, and very windy   d. sandstorm

5. very hot and dry for a long time   e. tornado

6. loud noise   f. heat wave

2 **Write the temperature change.**

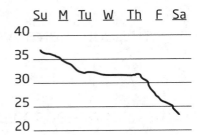 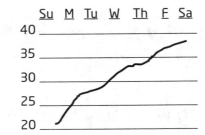 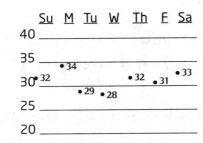

1. a _____ in temperature 2. a _____ in temperature 3. a _____ of temperatures

3 **Write true sentences.**

1. After you see thunder, you may hear lightning.
   After you see lightning, you may hear thunder.

2. A lot of rain after a flood can cause a drought.

   _____

3. It can be very hot during a blizzard or an ice storm.

   _____

4. The wind speed is slow in a tropical storm.

   _____

4 **Read.** Work with a partner. Student 1, go to page 122. Student 2, go to page 124.

5 **Listen.** Check T for *True* and F for *False*. **TR: 1.4**

1. Xavier puts on his winter coat if it snows.   Ⓣ   Ⓕ

2. If a blizzard is coming, Xavier goes to visit his aunt.   Ⓣ   Ⓕ

3. If a storm is coming, Berta listens to the radio.   Ⓣ   Ⓕ

4. If it snows, Berta watches TV.   Ⓣ   Ⓕ

6 **Write what the weather is going to be like.** Then explain what you normally do in that weather.

1.

It's going to rain. If it rains,

I always stay home.

2.

_____

_____

3.

_____

_____

4.

_____

_____

7 **Read and match.**

1. If there is lightning,

2. If the temperature drops and rises,

3. If a tropical storm comes,

4. If the wind speed is 120 kilometers per hour (74 miles),

5. If it's hot for two weeks,

6. If an ice storm comes,

a. the temperature drops.

b. it is a heat wave.

c. there is also thunder.

d. it is a hurricane.

e. there is a range of temperatures.

f. it will bring rain and high winds.

Copycat Animals

VOCABULARY 1

1 **Find and circle.** Hidden words are down and across.

W	F	G	Q	I	N	S	E	C	T	U	L	H	X	L
M	R	E	O	F	E	N	A	H	E	C	U	U	I	R
C	O	P	I	E	S	J	Z	A	N	P	O	N	O	F
A	D	W	A	F	P	A	P	R	E	D	A	T	O	R
M	I	D	G	Q	E	N	I	A	N	G	W	T	Y	I
O	H	B	H	I	C	S	U	C	E	B	O	J	V	G
U	B	O	I	M	I	T	A	T	E	S	Y	I	X	H
F	V	Q	D	I	E	S	K	E	R	P	O	B	O	T
L	S	R	E	C	S	M	U	R	P	O	L	K	R	E
A	T	K	A	P	U	E	J	I	E	T	K	U	H	N
G	O	S	T	R	I	P	E	S	O	S	I	T	P	A
E	C	D	X	E	I	J	R	T	U	A	V	T	E	Z
D	M	Q	S	Y	X	P	O	I	S	O	N	O	U	S
A	F	M	R	O	O	U	P	C	A	C	Y	I	Z	U
Z	A	M	H	E	C	R	E	S	E	M	B	L	E	X

camouflage	poisonous
characteristics	predator
copies	prey
frighten	resemble
hide	species
hunt	spots
imitates	stripes
insect	

2 **Read and write.** Use words from the puzzle.

1. It's hard to see some animals because of the marks on their bodies.

   The _____ on some animals can be used as _____.

2. A/An _____ uses camouflage so it doesn't frighten its

   _____ when it's time to hunt.

3. Some animals use color so other animals can't see them. A/An _____ that

   is green can _____ on a leaf.

3 Match. Make logical sentences.

1. Some insects have characteristics
2. A frog has two spots on its back
3. The tiger has stripes on its body
4. Predators try not to be seen when they hunt prey

a. that imitate eyes.
b. that can run or hide when frightened.
c. that help to camouflage it in a jungle.
d. that resemble other poisonous insects.

4 Listen for the puzzle words. Write the matching words under the photos. TR: 2.1

insect

camouflage _____

wasp

resembles _____

tiger

stripes_____

butterfly

spots_____

rabbit

hide _____

black widow spider

poisonous_____

5 Make sentences. Use at least two of these words in each sentence.

> camouflage   characteristics   copy   frighten   hunt   imitate   poisonous   resemble

1. _____
2. _____
3. _____

SONG

1 **Listen and write.** Choose sentences from the song for each picture. TR: 2.2

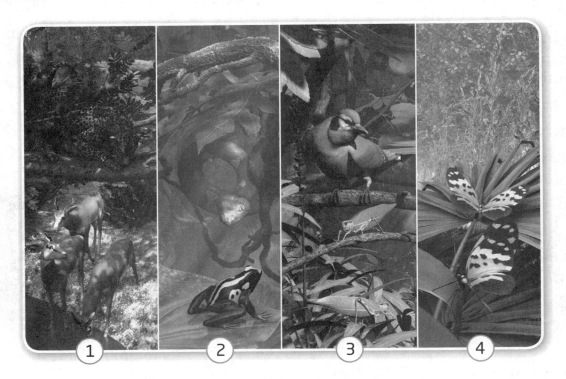

1. Predators are everywhere, and looking for a feast! _____

2. _____

3. _____

4. _____

2 **Listen to the song again and answer.** Choose words from the song.

1. What do a frog's stripes tell its enemies?

_____

2. Why do animals do amazing things?

_____

3. What must the predator and prey do each and every day?

_____

4. What do animals do to hide in front of our eyes?

_____

GRAMMAR 1

Comparisons with as . . . as

The striped frog	is		poisonous		a snake.
The red butterfly	isn't	as	pretty	as	the blue one.

as . . . as = The two things are the same.
not as . . . as = The two things are different.

1 **Complete the sentences.**

cute   dangerous   ~~fast~~   green   soft

1. A predator must be _____as fast as_____ its prey.

2. Some insects can be _____ a leaf.

3. The bite of a spider can be _____ the bite of a snake.

4. The fur of a fox is _____ a cat's fur.

5. I think a deer is _____ a dog.

2 **Write comparisons.**

1. the walk of a duck / funny / a turtle's walk
   The walk of a duck is as funny as a turtle's walk.

2. the wool of an alpaca / soft / a sheep's wool
   _____

3. jaguar / dangerous / a cougar
   _____

4. predator / can be / camouflaged / its prey
   _____

5. a bee sting / painful / a wasp sting
   _____

VOCABULARY 2

1 **Complete the sentences.** Some words will be used more than once.

attack   avoid   confuse   defend   escape

1. A bird goes underwater to _____ an attacking predator.

2. A zebra moves its head to _____ the kick of another zebra.

3. Lions _____ a buffalo.

4. A penguin turns to _____ its nest from a seal.

5. Fish swim in a circle around a hungry seal to _____ it.

6. A baby deer hides in the grass to _____ predators.

GRAMMAR 2

Tag questions

Positive			Negative	
The jaguar	**is**	endangered,	**isn't**	it?
Penguins	**are**	birds,	**aren't**	they?
That snake	**was**	a cobra,	**wasn't**	it?
Dinosaurs	**were**	reptiles,	**weren't**	they?
You	**eat**	meat,	**don't**	you?
A mongoose	**eats**	snakes,	**doesn't**	it?
The bears	**ate**	the fish,	**didn't**	they?

Negative			Positive	
This insect	**isn't**	poisonous,	**is**	it?
You	**aren't**	afraid of dogs,	**are**	you?
That snake	**wasn't**	dangerous,	**was**	it?
Those	**weren't**	dolphins,	**were**	they?
You	**don't** eat	meat,	**do**	you?
A giraffe	**doesn't** eat	meat,	**does**	it?
The bears	**didn't** eat	the fish,	**did**	they?

At the end, use a pronoun.

The jaguar is endangered, isn't it?

Penguins are birds, aren't they?

1 Read and write.

1. The colors are so beautiful, _____?

2. The spots on the wings look like eyes, _____?

3. That butterfly doesn't taste bad to predators, _____?

4. Well, I'm not going to find out myself, _____?

5. That's a better way of finding the answer to my question, _____?

2 Listen and say. Write the question. TR: 2.3

1. _____is it_____?

2. _____?

3. _____?

4. _____?

5. _____?

6. _____?

7. _____?

8. _____?

3 Listen. Check your answers to Activity 2. TR: 2.4

1 **Listen and read.** TR: 2.5

Why Do Mockingbirds Copy?

Mockingbirds live in North and South America. They are good copycats. They imitate other birds. But they can also imitate other animals. They can even make sounds that resemble a piano or car alarm. Mockingbirds learn to sing many songs. Some learn more than 200 different songs. They can often trick people! But they can't trick other birds. If mockingbirds can't trick other birds, why do they copy sounds? They do it to attract and avoid other birds!

Males are loud singers, and they sing many songs. They always sing when they want to meet females. A male bird can sing most of the day and night. The singing attracts females. But it also keeps away other males. The longer a mockingbird lives, the more songs it knows. To show this characteristic, the male mockingbird sings all the songs it knows. A female mockingbird is attracted to a male who has lived a long time.

Mockingbirds usually sing short songs. They sing each sound several times. Then they move to the next sound. Female mockingbirds sing softly and less often than males. They usually sing at their nests in the winter to keep away other birds. When another bird comes near, the mockingbird makes a loud noise to frighten it.

It's amazing that the mockingbird can copy so many songs of other birds. Some songs are not easy to learn. The mockingbird must listen well to imitate the sounds. But a mockingbird also has good eyes and a good memory. When a person comes near its nest, the mockingbird remembers that person. It knows that person's face after many years!

2 **Check T for *True* and F for *False*.**

1. The female mockingbird sings more often than the male. (T) (F)

2. When a mockingbird imitates, it often tricks other birds. (T) (F)

3. The female mockingbird sings to attract the male. (T) (F)

4. Mockingbirds can remember human beings. (T) (F)

3 Check what you learned from the text.

Mockingbird characteristic	Males	Females
1. Live in North and South America		
2. Imitate other birds and other animals		
3. Are loud singers		
4. Always sing many songs		
5. Sing to attract		
6. Sing to keep away other birds		

4 Write. List the facts that you know about the lives of mockingbirds. Use the text in Activity 1 and the chart in Activity 3.

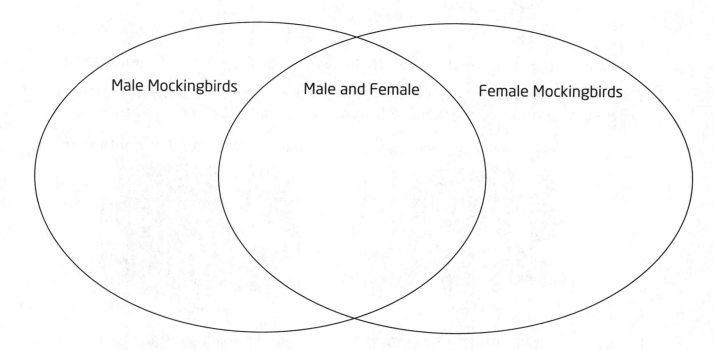

Male Mockingbirds   Male and Female   Female Mockingbirds

5 Write. Answer the questions in your notebook.

1. What is the most interesting fact you learned about mockingbirds?

2. What other animals can imitate sounds?

WRITING

1 **Read *Animals That Imitate* in your Student's Book.** How did the writer plan? Read the steps.

1. The writer chose a type of animal. The writer chose *copycat animals.*

2. Next, the writer described the characteristics. *Some animals copy the appearance or the sound of another animal.*

3. Then the writer wrote about specific animals and described how they copy.

4. Then the writer wrote a first sentence that says what the writing is about. *Some animals copy other animals to avoid attack.*

How do they look?	The viceroy and monarch butterflies resemble each other. The ash borer moth looks like a wasp.
How do they sound?	Termites make a hissing sound, like a snake. A dormouse does the same thing.
Do they have weapons?	The ash borer moth doesn't have a stinger like a wasp.

5. Next, the writer wrote about the characteristics of these types of animals.

6. Finally, the writer wrote sentences about specific animals. To show how these animals belong to a group, the writer used words such as *both, like,* and *but.*

Imitate the appearance

ash borer moth

wasp

Imitate the sound of another animal

dormouse

snake

2 **Plan to write about animals that have some of the same characteristics.** Take notes.

1. Choose a type of animal _____

2. Describe the characteristics all the animals share. Is it how they look? Is it how they sound? Is it what they can do?

_____

3 **Complete the chart.** Write the kind of characteristics you chose in the first column. Write the way the animals share each characteristic in the second column.

How they look	The animals resemble each other.

4 **Now follow steps 1-6 in Activity 1 to write your paragraphs in your notebook.**

5 **Write.** Choose one of the topics below, and write two or three paragraphs, using classification. Plan your writing, and follow the steps in Activity 1. Write in your notebook.

- cats and dogs
- apples and oranges
- pens and pencils

UNIT 2 REVIEW

1 **Do the puzzle.** Find the hidden word.

camouflage   characteristics   copies
frighten   hide   hunt   imitates
insect   poisonous   predator   prey
resembles   species   spots   stripes

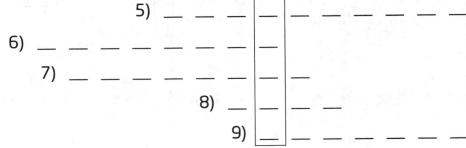

Hidden word: _____

1. To a hungry lion, an antelope is _____.

2. One butterfly species _____ the color of another species that tastes bad.

3. This animal is often green or brown and is prey for birds.

4. _____ are round shapes on skin or fur that help camouflage an animal.

5. An animal uses _____ to make it hard to see.

6. A lion walks quietly so that it doesn't _____ its prey.

7. This is an animal that attacks and eats other animals.

8. A hawk flies in a circle to _____ for mice.

9. _____ are long marks on animals.

2 **Ask and answer.** Work with a partner. Student 1, go to page 122. Student 2, go to page 124.

3 Complete the sentences.

clear   sharp   ~~slippery~~   sweet   tall

1. A frog is ___as slippery as___ a snake, ___isn't it___?

2. The water of some lakes is _____ glass, _____?

3. He likes fruit that is _____ candy, _____?

4. Your sister is _____ my sister, _____?

5. The teeth of a shark can be _____ a knife, _____?

4 Read and write.

1. some actors are / famous / the movies they make
   Some actors are as famous as the movies they make, aren't they?

2. his idea is / good / hers

   _____

3. an earache is / bad / a headache

   _____

4. comic books are / fun to read / any book

   _____

5. that blizzard was / cold / an ice storm

   _____

Unit 3
Music in Our World

VOCABULARY 1

1 **Look and listen.** Write the words that you hear. TR: 3.1

band	beat	chord	concert	drum	~~flute~~	guitar	lead singer
melody	note	perform	piano	~~practice~~	rhythm	saxophone	violin

1. _____practice_____
   _____flute_____

2. _____
   _____

3. _____
   _____

4. _____
   _____

5. _____
   _____

6. _____
   _____

7. _____
   _____

8. _____
   _____

2 Unscramble and write.

So you want to start a band? If you are a good singer, you could be the *dlae nregsi*

_____. You'll also need someone who plays the *msurd* _____

to make the *tbae* _____ for the group. To make the *mythhr*

_____, you'll need someone who can play *srodch* _____

on the *rtaugi* _____. The *entso* _____ of the *yoldme*

_____ can be played on the *opnai* _____, the *hoopnxase*

_____ , or the *oliivn* _____ . You'll need to *tarpccie*

_____ a lot if you want the music to sound great. One day you might be

good enough to *rorpfem* _____ at a *ecctnor* _____.

3 Read the words in the box. Write the words in the correct column.

beat   chord   drum   flute   guitar   melody   note   piano   saxophone   violin

Instruments		Parts of Music	

4 Underline the best answer.

1. play an instrument for others to hear (perform / practice)
2. play an instrument to get better at it (perform / practice)
3. a thing used to make music (lead singer / instrument)
4. a person who uses the voice to make music (lead singer / instrument)

SONG

1 **Listen to the song.** Answer the song questions in order. TR: 3.2

1. Have you ever listened to _____hip-hop_____ ?

   Yes, I have. / No, I haven't. _____

2. Have you ever listened to _____?

   _____

3. I can hear the _____. Can you?

   _____

4. Have you ever played a _____?

   _____

5. Have you ever played a _____?

   _____

6. Have you ever played a _____?

   _____

2 **Read and write.** Write new verses for the song.

Listen to the rhythm.   Listen to the _____.

Listen to that band!   Listen to that _____!

Sing the notes   Sing the _____

and clap your hands.   and _____.

The flute is playing.   The _____ is playing.

The piano is, too.   The _____ is, too.

I can hear the guitar.   I can hear the _____.

Can you?   Can you?

GRAMMAR 1

Present perfect with *ever* and *never*

Question				Answer	
Have	you	ever	**played**	the piano?	Yes, I **have**. Yes, I**'ve played** it many times.	I've = I have haven't = have not
					No, I **haven't**. No, I**'ve** <u>never</u> **played** the piano.	
Has	she		**been**	to a concert?	Yes, she **has**. Yes, she's **been** to a concert once.	she's = she has hasn't = has not
					No, she **hasn't**. No, she's <u>never</u> **been** to a concert.	

once = one time
never = at no time in the past

1 **Read and write.**

1. Have we ever been there?
No, <u>we have never been there</u> .

2. _____
No, she has never listened to a flute.

3. _____
No, he has never played a chord on the guitar.

4. _____
No, I have never been to a concert.

5. Have they ever practiced together? No, _____ .

2 **Read and write.** Write your own sentences.

1. This is the first time my teacher _____ .

2. It's the only time I _____ .

3. That's the first time my friends _____ .

4. This is the only time my brother _____ .

3 **Write three questions beginning with *Have you ever* . . .**
Then work with a partner. Take turns to ask and answer your questions.

> Have you ever written a song before?

> No, I have never written a song before!

VOCABULARY 2

1 **Look and match.** Write the name of the type of music. Then write the names of performers you know in each column.

> classical   hip-hop   jazz   pop   rock

1.
_____

2.
_____

3.
_____

4.
_____

5.
_____

hip-hop	classical	rock	jazz	pop

2 **Listen.** Number the music styles in the order you hear them. **TR: 3.3**

○ classical   ○ hip-hop   ○ jazz   ○ pop   ○ rock

GRAMMAR 2

Comparative adverbs

She	runs	**faster**	**than**			I do.
	sings	**better**				
He	plays	**more**	**beautifully**	**than**		
	practices		**often**			

She	runs		**fast**		**as**	I do.
	sings	**as**	**well**			
He	plays		**beautifully**			
	practices		**often**			

Irregular forms: *well* → *better (than)*   *badly* → *worse (than)*
With *often*, you can use *more* or *less*: *He practices <u>more often</u> / <u>less often</u> than I do.*

1 **Complete the sentences.**

1. He can perform _____ the other musicians if he practices. (=, well)
2. She plays classical music _____ pop music. (-, often)
3. He plays the violin _____ he plays other string instruments. (+, well)
4. He moves his right hand _____ his left hand. (+, fast)
5. I play the guitar _____ I play the bass. (-, frequently)

2 **Read and write.** Write sentences using comparisons.

1. Hsin plays the piano well. Hua plays the piano better.
   Hua plays the piano better than Hsin.

2. He practices the first song often. He practices the last song less often.
   _____
   _____

3. We can sing well. They can sing well.
   _____

4. I like to listen to rock music. I like to listen to hip-hop music a little less.
   _____
   _____

5. Pang goes to concerts two times per year. Ming goes to concerts three times per year.
   _____
   _____

1 **Listen and read.** TR: 3.4

Listen to This!

"Hey, turn that music down!"

Do you ever wonder why your parents tell you to turn the volume down when you're listening to loud music? It's not because they don't like the rhythm and melody. (Well, your favorite music might not be their favorite music!) It's important to listen to music and other sounds at the right volume because if you don't, it can hurt your ears!

Did you know that sound travels in waves? These waves can move quickly or slowly, depending on their frequency. The type of sound that these waves make when they move is called *pitch.* If a sound wave moves slowly, the pitch is low, like the sound of someone playing a bass guitar. If a sound wave moves quickly, the pitch is high, like the sound of someone playing a flute or violin.

Sometimes, a sound has a frequency that is too high or too low for people to hear. We measure frequency in hertz. The range that humans can hear is 20–20,000 hertz (Hz). Dolphins can hear sounds from 75 to 200,000 Hz! That means they can hear things we can't.

We measure the volume of a sound in decibels (dB). The sound of people whispering is about 30 dB, the sound of a rock concert is closer to 115 dB, and the sound of a jet engine is about 140 dB! The max output of most phones and digital music players is between 70 and 90 dB, which is really loud! Try to keep the volume at 50 dB instead. Your ears will thank you!

Elephant	Dog	Dolphin
5–10,000 Hz	10–60,000 Hz	75–200,000 Hz

2. Check T for *True* and F for *False*.

1. Sound travels in waves.   (T)   (F)

2. If a sound wave moves slowly, the pitch is high.   (T)   (F)

3. A violin has a higher pitch than a bass guitar.   (T)   (F)

4. People can hear higher pitches than dolphins can hear.   (T)   (F)

3. Correct the false sentences in Activity 2.

_____

_____

_____

4. Match the words to the definitions.

1. pitch
2. frequency
3. decibel
4. hertz

a. unit used to measure frequency
b. the position of a sound in a range from low to high
c. the speed at which sound waves move
d. unit used to measure the volume of a sound

5. Label the graph.

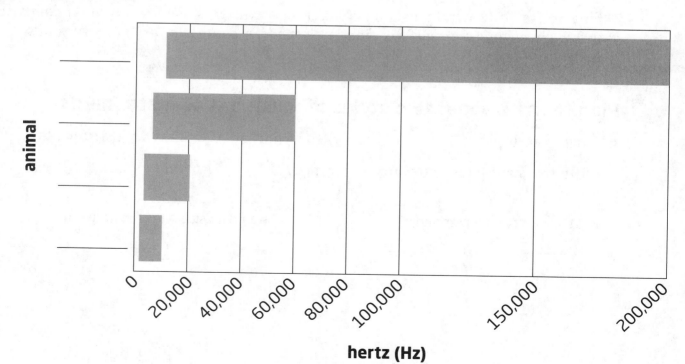

animal

hertz (Hz)

0   20,000   40,000   60,000   80,000   100,000   150,000   200,000

WRITING

1 **Read *Composing, Then and Now* in your Student's Book.** How did the writer plan? Read the steps.

1. The writer chose the topic of composing.

2. Next, the writer chose a contrast in that topic: composing in the past and composing now.

3. Then the writer wrote different facts about the past and now.

Composing Then	Composing Now
1. Composers used pen and paper.	1. Composers use computer and phone apps.
2. Composers wrote notes on lined measures of music.	2. Composers hum a song and the app writes the notes.

4. The writer chose words of contrast to show differences: *but now, before, instead, in the past, while.*

5. Next, the writer wrote an opening paragraph describing what happened in the past and finished the paragraph with a contrasting sentence about the present. *In the past, composers wrote down their music with paper and a pen. But now, . . .*

6. Then the writer contrasted other characteristics of composing in the past and composing now.

7. Finally, the writer wrote a sentence to close the text. *While a traditional composer was busy cleaning ink off his fingers, a modern composer writes more songs instead!*

2 **Plan to write about two styles of music or two instruments.**

1. Circle your topic.   two styles of music   two instruments

2. Write the main facts you want to contrast.

First music style or instrument	Second music style or instrument
_____	_____
1.	1.
2.	2.

3 **Choose words of contrast to show differences.** Use them to contrast the information in the chart.

1. _____
   _____

2. _____
   _____

4 **Write more characteristics of the things you are contrasting.**

First style or musical instrument

1. _____
2. _____
3. _____

Second style or musical instrument

1. _____
2. _____
3. _____

5 **Now follow steps 2-7 in Activity 1.** Write your text describing contrast in your notebook.

6 **Express yourself.** Choose a topic below to write about *then* and *now*. Plan your writing and follow the steps in Activity 1. Write your new text in your notebook.

Cooking meals, then and now   Going somewhere, then and now

Having fun, then and now   Using a phone, then and now

UNIT 3 REVIEW

1 **Read and write.** Read the second paragraph on page 40 of your Student's Book. Write the words under the fish. Put them in order.

beat   chord   melody   note   rhythm

rhythm

2 **Complete the sentences.**

band   concert   lead singer   practice   rhythm   saxophone

1. You can be a _____.

2. You can start a _____ with others.

3. You can _____ to get better.

4. You can go to a _____.

3 **Choose and write.** Choose two words from the box. Write a sentence with the two words.

band   beat   classical   concert   drum   flute   guitar
hip-hop   jazz   lead singer   perform   pop   rock   saxophone

1. _I want to play the guitar in a rock band!_____

2. _____

3. _____

4. _____

5. _____

4 Read and write. Complete the sentences with words from the box.

> better   better than   ever   ever been   more often than   never

Have you _____ sad and listened to music to make you happy? Few

things work _____ music to change how we feel. Many people have

a special song or piece of music. When they are feeling sad, they want to hear it

_____ any other music. Has this _____ happened to you? If this

has _____ happened to you, try listening to different songs next time you

feel unhappy. Perhaps you will find one that works _____ than any other to

change your mood.

5 Listen and write. TR: 3.5

1. Has Raul ever played that beat faster than Maria? _No, he hasn't._____

2. Have you ever heard me play louder? _____

3. Has he ever practiced as much as this week? _____

4. Does Roberto ever play music softer? _____

5. Does Carmen ever sing worse than Alexa? _____

6 Write three things that you have never done. Then find someone in the class who has never done the things below.

ride a bike _____   play basketball _____

have cereal for breakfast _____   listen to hip-hop _____

go to a classical concert _____   sleep until eleven _____

Markus, have you ever ridden a bike?

Yes, I have!

Alex, have you ever ridden a bike?

No, I haven't.

Review: Units 1–3

1 **Match.** Connect the words that have opposite meanings. Then label the pictures.

1. rise
2. hunt
3. predator
4. drought
5. attack
6. ice storm

a. flood
b. hide
c. defend
d. heat wave
e. drop
f. prey

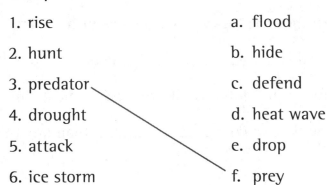

_____   _____   _____

_____ predator – prey _____   _____   _____

2 **Read and write.** Complete the sentences with true information.

1. If a species copies another species, <u>it imitates it</u>.

2. If I listen to classical music, _____.

3. If a rabbit sees a fox, _____.

4. If the beat of the music is fast, _____.

5. If a snake has stripes, _____.

6. If she is the lead singer, _____.

3 **Read, look, and listen.** Match. Then number the pictures. TR: 3.6

1. The dog is

2. The storm is not

3. If it's a hip-hop concert,

4. He explains that ice storms are

5. If the cat attacks the insect,

6. She thinks the sound of the guitar is not

a. she always goes.

b. as nice as playing the piano.

c. more confused than frightened.

d. as strong as a blizzard.

e. he's not going to watch.

f. as bad as a hurricane.

g. as nice as the sound of a violin.

h. very common during the winter.

4 **Answer the questions.** Use words from the box.

> attack   concert   escape   hurricane   piano   thunder

1. Why are we going to evacuate? _There's going to be a hurricane._

2. What instrument is she going to play? _____

3. Why is the tiger hiding in a tree near the zebra? _____

4. What are we going to hear after we see lightning? _____

5. When is the band going to practice? _____

6. What is the zebra going to do if it sees a predator? _____

5 **Read the text and write the missing words.** Write one word on each line.

Example   Have you _____ever_____ wanted to learn a
           musical instrument, but you're not sure which
           one? There are so many different instruments, it's
1   hard to choose, _____ it?
2   There are three main _____ of
3   instruments: string, _____,
           and percussion. If you want to play a
           string instrument like a violin, you're going
4   _____ need a lot of practice! At first,
5   it may be harder to play _____ a guitar,
           for example.
                Do you have a good sense of rhythm? You
           may like to try playing the drums. But they're
6   not quiet, _____ they? If you want
7   something you can play _____ quietly, a
           flute may be the instrument for you.
                Don't forget to practice your new instrument
8   every day, and you'll soon play _____.
           Have fun!

6 **Read.** Check T for *True* and F for *False*.

This octopus needs to hunt, but it must avoid being hunted. If it is attacked, it first tries to escape. It can shoot water out of its body. The water pushes it at a fast speed through the sea. If the predator follows, the octopus can shoot out black ink. The confused predator can't see, and the octopus escapes. Then the octopus tries to hide. It sometimes hides under the sand with only its eyes peeking out. It also changes color to match its shelter. In some cases, an octopus will leave an arm behind! The arm still moves in the water and attracts the hunter. The octopus escapes. In six weeks, it grows a new arm, but the new arm has no bones! An octopus has no bones at all!

1. The octopus doesn't hunt.   (T) (F)

2. The octopus moves in the water by shooting black ink.   (T) (F)

3. The octopus can change its color.   (T) (F)

4. The octopus will sometimes break a bone in its arm and leave it behind.   (T) (F)

5. In six weeks, the octopus can grow a new arm.   (T) (F)

7 **Read and write the answer.** Use information from Activity 6.

1. What does an octopus do to escape from a predator?

_____

2. An octopus is smart. What do you know about an octopus that says it's smart?

_____

3. An octopus hunts. What kind of animal is it?

_____

8 **Write.** A shark will hunt an octopus for food. What can happen if a shark finds an octopus? Write a short story. Use what you learned in Activity 6.

_____

_____

_____

_____

Life Out There

VOCABULARY 1

1 **Do a puzzle.** Read the clues. Fill in the words.

atmosphere
comet
data
debate
extraterrestrials
galaxy
journey
orbit
planet
solar system
space
universe

Across

1. People _____ whether there is life beyond Earth.

6. Mars travels in a(n) _____ around the sun.

7. Information = _____

10. Earth is the third _____ from the sun.

11. The _____ is made of space and all the stars.

12. Earth's _____ is like a blanket that protects us.

Down

2. If _____ exist, they live in other places beyond Earth.

3. A(n) _____ is a trip from one place to another.

4. The _____ is made up of the sun and the planets that go around it.

5. We sent rockets into _____.

8. A big group of stars is known as a(n) _____.

9. A(n) _____ is a moving cloud of rock, ice, and gas.

2 Complete the sentences.

atmosphere	data	debate
extraterrestrials	orbit	solar system

1. Venus is a planet in our _____.

2. Venus travels around the sun in a closer _____ than Earth.

3. Venus has a(n) _____ that hides the planet's surface.

4. Scientists have sent instruments to Venus to collect _____.

5. Do you think _____ can live on Venus?

6. You believe it and I don't. We can _____ the topic to decide who is right.

3 Write. Write words to describe these things. Then work with a partner. Ask and answer.

How can you describe . . .

1. an extraterrestrial? _____

2. space? _____

3. an orbit? _____

4. a comet? _____

5. the universe? _____

SONG

1 **Listen to the song.** Match to complete. **TR: 4.1**

1. But right here on planet Earth,   a. deep in outer space.

2. Let's all take a journey   b. where flowers grow.

3. We might find things   c. life is all around.
   we've never seen

4. We might find a moon   d. far away from here.

5. Beyond our solar system,   e. past the atmosphere.

2 **Read and match.** Write a sentence from Activity 1 that matches each picture.

1. _____

2. _____

3. _____

3 **Listen and write.** Listen to track 4.1 again. List some things the song says we might find. Then write a new verse!

1. We might find _____ a moon _____.

2. We might find _____.

3. We might find _____.

4. We might find _____.

_____

_____

_____

GRAMMAR 1

May and might

There	**may**	(not)	be	life on other planets.
We	**might**		travel	to other planets in the future.

You can use *may* and *might* to talk about the present or the future. They mean the same thing.

1 **Write sentences with *may/might* that say you're not sure.**

1. We have a debate tomorrow. _We may/might have a debate tomorrow._

2. That star has planets. _____

3. The universe is bigger than you think. _____

4. The comet's orbit goes outside the solar system. _____
_____

5. That planet has an atmosphere. _____

2 **Read and write.** Use the word(s) in parentheses to finish each sentence.

1. We heard that extraterrestrials (*live*) _might live on other planets_.

2. I see that a planet (*be next to*) _____.

3. He knows that a comet (*fly across*) _____.

4. She thought that the debate (*end*) _____.

5 I think that the data (*not be*) _____.

3 **Write.** In your notebook, write three questions about what your partner might do tonight. Then ask and answer with your partner. Answer to say you're not sure. Take turns.

> Will you look for comets in the sky tonight?

> I might look for comets in the sky tonight.

VOCABULARY 2

1 **Read and look.** Match each picture with a sentence.

1. The rocket fires and lifts the spacecraft away from Earth.

2. The astronaut searches her instruments.

3. An astronaut at the space station communicates with scientists.

2 **Read and write.**

astronaut   communicate   search   spacecraft   space station

1. You _____ to find something.

2. You _____ when you want to tell someone something.

3. A(n) _____ is a person who travels in space.

4. The _____ orbits Earth, and people live and work in it.

5. A(n) _____ carries people into space and back.

3 **Solve the riddles.** Choose the word pair that matches the description in each riddle.

astronaut/rocket   search/communicate   spacecraft/space station

1. You can do one of these things alone. The other thing needs two or more people.

   _____

2. You can be one of these things. You can travel inside the other thing.

   _____

3. You can travel inside one of these things. You can live in the other thing.

   _____

GRAMMAR 2

Indefinite pronouns

Everyone in this class speaks English. We all speak English.

Someone took my pencil, but I don't know who.

I don't know **anyone** in this class.
Does **anyone** want to be an astronaut?

No one went to school yesterday. It was a holiday.

Use *anyone* in negative sentences and questions.
I *don't* know **anyone** in this class. (Not: ~~I don't know no one in this class.~~)
Does **anyone** want to be an astronaut?

1 **Look and write.** Tell about the picture.

anyone   everyone   no one   someone

Jiao   Lan   Gao   Zhuang

1. _____ is sitting down.

2. Maybe _____ told a joke because Gao is laughing.

3. I don't see _____ wearing a helmet.

4. _____ is dressed as an astronaut.

2 **Read and write.** Use the words from Activity 1 to complete each sentence.

1. I will be the only one home. _____ else will be at work or school.

2. Be careful with your book. Don't give it to _____.

3. It is very late. _____ is on the phone at this hour.

4. I don't know if it's Hugo or Luis, but I hear _____ calling my name.

3 **Listen and circle the answer.** TR: 4.2

1. *Everyone / Someone* wants to go to the planetarium.

2. *Someone / No one* saw the comet.

3. *Anyone / Someone* can answer that question.

4. I want to invite *someone / everyone* to come with me.

1 Listen and read. TR: 4.3

Life on Mars

Mars is the fourth planet from the sun. You can see Mars without a telescope, but you need a telescope to see its characteristics. Many years ago, people began looking at Mars with telescopes. They wondered if Mars ever had life.

In 1877, an Italian scientist, Giovanni Schiaparelli, saw strange lines on the surface of Mars and wrote about them. Some people read what Schiaparelli had written and thought the lines were canals. A canal is a waterway that's man made. They thought that Martians may have made them!

When telescopes got better, people forgot the canal idea. In 1965, the spacecraft *Mariner 4* flew by Mars and took photos. The photos showed that the surface looks like Earth's moon, with marks from rocks hitting it.

In 2012, the first Mars rover *Curiosity* landed on Mars. It sent data back to Earth. Since then, many other spacecraft have been sent to fly past, orbit, or land on Mars. We have learned a lot more about Mars. One recent discovery is exciting. For years, scientists looked for liquid water on Mars. They found small amounts of ice. But in 2018, they discovered an underground lake, 19 km (12 mi.) long. Scientists think there may be other similar lakes on Mars.

Scientists have not found life on Mars yet. But some think that where there is water, there may be life, or life may have been there many years ago. In 2018, the InSight mission landed on Mars. Its aim is to study deep down below the surface of Mars. It will investigate the structure of the planet and look for earthquakes—or rather marsquakes! Scientists hope to learn about the origins of Mars, as well as other planets in the solar system.

2 Check T for *True* and F for *False*.

1. Mars has canals that are like rivers.   T   F
2. In 1877, *Mariner 4* flew by Mars and took photos.   T   F
3. Scientists have discovered a lake on the surface of Mars.   T   F
4. Scientists don't know if there was ever life on Mars.   T   F

3 Read and write.

1. You can see Mars without a _____.

2. People thought that they saw _____ on Mars, but they were wrong.

3. The surface of Mars has marks from falling rocks like Earth's _____.

4. It's possible that there was _____ on Mars many years ago.

4 Complete the chart. Use information from Activity 1.

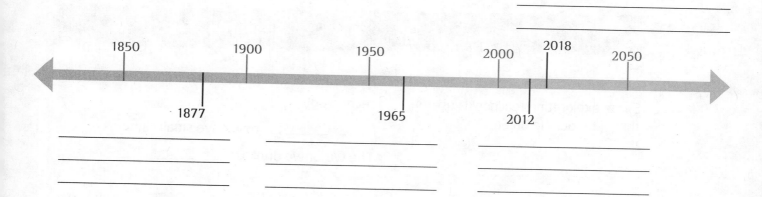

_____
_____

1850   1900   1950   2000   2018   2050

1877   1965   2012

_____ _____ _____
_____ _____ _____
_____ _____ _____

5 Read and answer. Use information from Activity 1.

1. What are canals? _____

2. Mars does not have canals. What helped people learn this?

   _____

3. Why does the land on Mars look like Earth's moon?

   _____

4. What exciting discovery have scientists made recently?

   _____

6 Write and discuss. In your notebook, note one fact for each of the following. Then compare notes with a partner and discuss.

• Something you already knew about Mars.

• Something you just learned about Mars.

• Something you'd like to learn about Mars.

WRITING

1 **Read *Exploring Space* in your Student's Book.** How did the writer plan? Read the steps below.

1. First, the writer chose an opinion. What was the writer's opinion?

   Space exploration takes time and money, but _____

   _____

   _____

2. Second, the writer wrote down persuasive facts that support the opinion.

Opinion	Supporting Facts
Space exploration teaches us useful things for our life on Earth.	Many _____ come from space technology. _____ now have small cameras. The water we drink is _____.

3. Third, the writer wrote persuasive expressions to introduce the facts. Look for the following expressions in the story.

   The facts show, according to experts

4. Fourth, the writer wrote a strong conclusion.

   I believe that searching for life in space is a good thing, too. It helps us to see how special our lives on Earth are.

5. Finally, the writer organized the sentences in a draft, or a first version, of the passage. The writer started with an introduction to the main idea.

   Main idea: *People spend a lot of time and money on space exploration.*

   Another good way of starting is to use an example to introduce a topic. You can decide to start with an example or with an introduction to the main idea.

   Example: *Without space exploration, many inventions such as the cameras on our smartphones might not exist.*

2 **Should we search for life in space?** Look at *Listening for Life* in your Student's Book. Write what you think. Should we search for life in space or not?

_____

_____

3 **Follow steps 2-5 in Activity 1.** Use the space below to plan. Then write your paragraphs in your notebook.

Opinions	Supporting Facts

Write expressions that introduce:

_____

Write a strong conclusion:

_____

4 **Write.** Choose one of the topics below, and write two or three paragraphs that persuade. Plan your writing, and follow the steps in Activity 1. Write your new paragraphs in your notebook.

There may (or may not) be life on other planets.

It may be good (or bad) for people to find life on other planets.

Space exploration helps (or doesn't help) people on Earth.

Learning about other planets is (or is not) important for people on Earth.

UNIT 4 REVIEW

1 **Read.** Underline the correct words.

1. Two planets in our *universe / solar system* orbit the sun closer than Earth.

2. A *comet / planet* may need an atmosphere to support life.

3. We use radios to *communicate / journey* with spacecraft.

4. Scientists collect *search / data* to look for life on other planets.

5. Astronauts use a spacecraft to get to the *rocket / space station*.

6. We have sent *astronauts / extraterrestrials* into space.

7. Scientists use SETI to *search / debate* for extraterrestrial intelligence.

8. Some *spacecraft / comets* have big orbits that go outside of the solar system.

2 **Read.** Draw lines to match.

1. Let's take a journey   a. with atmospheres.

2. Let's use a rocket   b. to send up our spacecraft.

3. Let's travel past   c. communicate back to Earth.

4. Let's find new data to   d. about extraterrestrials!

5. Let's search for planets   e. into space.

6. Let's end the debate   f. the moon and the planets.

3 **Read and write.** Use each word twice to complete the sentences.

debate   orbit   search

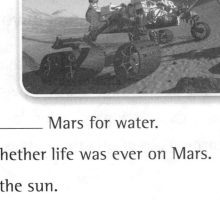

1. Two moons _____ the planet Mars.

2. Scientists look for data in their _____ for intelligent life.

3. The Mars rover, called *Curiosity*, may _____ Mars for water.

4. Scientists do not agree. They _____ whether life was ever on Mars.

5. You can see Mars in its _____ around the sun.

6. You can go to the _____ and say that Mars never had life on it.

4 **Look and listen.** Number the words in the order you first hear them. **TR: 4.4**

○ anyone

○ everyone

○ no one

○ someone

○ may

5 **Listen again.** Answer each question with a sentence. **TR: 4.5**

1. Who might come as an extraterrestrial?

_____

2. Who can people at the party dress like?

_____

3. What is the boy worried about?

_____

4. Who may come, too?

_____

6 **Ask and answer.** Work with a partner. Student 1, go to page 123 and ask a question. Student 2, go to page 125 and say the matching sentence. Take turns.

Can everyone see the comet in the sky?

We may all be able to see it if the sky is not cloudy.

Unit 5

Arts Lost and Found

VOCABULARY 1

1 **Read and write.** Choose the word that best describes each list of words.

> art   community   ~~culture~~   language   traditions

1. education, laws, music, clothing, beliefs _____culture_____

2. Spanish, Arabic, Chinese, Japanese _____

3. painting, drawing, coloring _____

4. stores, hospitals, schools, sports teams _____

5. cooking for holidays, singing songs, telling stories _____

2 **Read and complete the sentences.**

> hold on   passed down   proud   share

1. I feel good about my family. I am _____ of my family.

2. My father is a farmer. I want to be a farmer, too. When I'm older, I hope the farm is _____ to me by my father.

3. I cut my apple in half to give some to my sister. I _____ my apple with my sister.

4. My family sings together every Sunday. I want to _____ to that tradition and continue to sing every Sunday.

3 Label the pictures. Match the words to each picture.

art   hold on   share   storytelling   tourists   weave

_____

_____

_____

_____

_____

_____

4 Listen and write. Write the words in the order you hear them. TR: 5.1

art   community   culture   future   generation
language   local   proud   traditions

1. _____

4. _____

7. _____

2. _____

5. _____

8. _____

3. _____

6. _____

9. _____

5 What can you say? Use the words to write sentences.

1. future / art _I think about the future of art in our country._____

2. pass down / traditions _____

3. storytelling / share _____

4. tourists / weave _____

5. hold on / culture _____

SONG

1 **Listen.** Use the words in the box to complete the verses. TR: 5.2

> art   culture   family   holding on   pride   storytelling   weaving

Knowing your history is important.

_____ to your culture is an excellent thing!

Knowing your history is important.

It's up to you to keep your _____ strong!

What special _____ does your culture bring to our world?

What special thing does your _____ bring to our world?

_____? Learn to do it!

_____? Learn to tell it!

What brings your culture _____?

2 **Listen.** Check T for *True* and F for *False*. TR: 5.3

1. It isn't very important to know your history. (T) (F)

2. You don't need to keep your culture strong. (T) (F)

3. Culture can bring art to the world. (T) (F)

4. You learn to sew to do embroidery. (T) (F)

3 **Remember and write.** List three things from the song you can learn. Then write two new lines for the song.

1. Learn to sculpt it! _____sculpture_____

2. Learn to tell it! _____

3. Learn to sew it! _____

4. Learn to do it! _____

_____

_____

GRAMMAR 1

Gerunds as subjects

Running		is	good exercise.
Writing		takes	time to learn.
Taking	photos	is	fun.
Passing down	family stories	connects	generations.

run + -ing → running
write + -ing → writing
take + -ing → taking
pass down + -ing → passing
down

1 **Read.** Complete the sentences.

communicate   debate   ~~hold on~~   pass down   search

1. _____Holding on_____ to traditions is very important!
2. _____ my grandfather's clock to me made my father happy.
3. _____ by telephone is harder in another language.
4. _____ for a good song to sing is exciting.
5. _____ is one way to learn how someone else thinks.

2 **Write.** What about you? Complete each sentence about you and your friends or family.

1. Walking _____.
2. Writing _____.
3. Watching TV _____.
4. Cleaning _____.
5. Eating _____.
6. Drawing _____.

3 **Read and complete.**   making   painting   storytelling   weaving   writing

The Orkney Islands, off the north coast of Scotland, have a proud history and culture. _____ beautiful things has always been important to the people of the islands. _____ is a traditional activity there, using wool from the local sheep. Many artists live and work on the islands.

_____, pottery, and jewelry making are all traditional activities kept alive today. The traditional stories of the islands are celebrated, too. _____ events and festivals are held regularly. _____ stories down is another way of passing them down to future generations.

VOCABULARY 2

1 **Read and look.** Match each word with a picture.

embroidery
handcrafted
jewelry making
pottery
sculpture

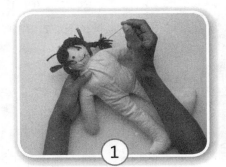

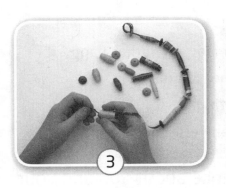

2 **Read and complete.** Use words from Activity 1.

When you're traveling, try to visit a local craft market. It's a great way to find out about another country's culture. It's very special to buy a beautiful object that has been _____ by a local person. Many countries have their own _____ traditions, using clay to make products such as vases and _____ of animals and people. If you like rings and necklaces, everywhere there are different traditions of _____. Or if you want to buy something special to wear, look for clothes with colorful _____. Alternatively, in some places you can take a class in a local craft, and take home something you have made yourself!

GRAMMAR 2

Gerunds as objects

I	like	playing the piano. cooking with my mom.	
	enjoy		
	love		
	tried		

I'm	good at	playing	the piano.
She's	interested in	learning	Japanese.
We're	excited about	visiting	Disneyland.
They're	tired of	studying	a lot.

verb + -*ing* word: *I like / enjoy / love / tried* playing the piano.
be + **adjective** + **preposition** + -*ing* word: *I am good at* playing the piano.

1 **Look and write.** Tell about the pictures.

good at/hit   likes/play   enjoys/make

loves/swim   interested in/learn   excited about/go

She is good at hitting
the ball.

_____
_____

_____
_____

_____
_____

_____
_____

_____
_____

1 Listen and read. TR: 5.4

Chinese Paper Art

Paper cutting or tearing is a cultural tradition in China. For centuries, it has been passed down from one generation to the next, especially from mothers to daughters. This beautiful art created by skillful artists is used to decorate doors, ceilings, and beds in people's homes, or at celebrations such as birthdays and weddings. At Chinese New Year, *window flowers* are glued to windows, creating beautiful patterns of light and shadow.

The two main techniques used are cutting the paper using a knife or scissors, or tearing it by hand. If the paper is cut, the edges are very smooth. Paper cutting can produce very fine and delicate work. This type of work is typical of southern China. If the paper is torn by hand, the edges are more simple and natural. Tearing is used more in northeast China. In addition, different parts of China have their own motifs—or pictures. These motifs can express many stories, ideas, and emotions.

It can be hard to hold on to traditions like these because young people don't know much about traditional art. Often they prefer spending their time on newer pastimes. The experts are getting older. If young people don't learn the traditions, they won't be able to pass them down to their own children. But recently there is a change. There are more exhibitions of traditional art. Artists are going into schools to teach children how to do paper cutting. Children enjoy working together with artists and talking to them about the meaning of their art. In this way, they are becoming proud of their culture and traditions.

2 **Read.** Check T for *True* or F for *False*.

1. Chinese paper art is a very old tradition.
2. Paper art is only used to decorate people's bedrooms.
3. Paper cutting is the same in every part of China.
4. Children in schools now like learning how to do paper art.

3 Label the pictures.

> a paper cutting artist   torn paper art   a window flower

1 _____

2 _____

3 _____

4 Write. Complete the chart. What are the differences?

Cut paper art	Torn paper art

5 Read and answer. Then work with a partner. Compare and discuss your answers.

1. In the past, paper art was mostly done by women and girls. Why do you think this was?

   _____

2. How much equipment do you need for paper cutting or tearing? Is it an expensive hobby?

   _____

3. Do you think Chinese paper art is difficult or easy to do? Why?

   _____

4. Do you think the tradition of paper art will continue in China for future generations?

   _____

WRITING

 Read *Cecilia's Blog* in your Student's Book. How did the writer plan her writing? Read the steps below.

1. First, the writer chose a topic. What was the topic? _____

2. Second, the writer wrote a step-by-step description of what she did.

a. took a long train ride

b. took a bus

c. the bus went up the mountain

d. arrived at Machu Picchu

e. climbed the stairs to the Sun Gate

f. stopped to rest

g. could see everything at the top

3. Third, the writer wrote her thoughts and feelings: *It was awesome, I was excited, It was so cool, I was incredibly tired, What a view, fabulous.*

4. Fourth, the writer asked the reader to post a response.

   What did the writer ask the reader? _____

5. Finally, the writer wrote a sentence of introduction and organized the sentences in a draft, or a first version, of the blog.

   My family and I went to Machu Picchu in Peru.

2 **Write a blog.** Look at Activity 2 in your Student's Book. Choose a topic about a family vacation or a special day.

_____

3 Follow steps 2-5 in Activity 1. Use the space below to plan. Write your blog entry in your notebook.

a. _____   b. _____

c. _____   d. _____

e. _____   f. _____

g. _____

Write your thoughts and feelings: _____

Write a sentence that asks for a response: _____

4 **Express yourself.** Choose one of the topics below, and write a blog entry. Plan your writing, and follow the steps in Activity 1. Write your new blog entry in your notebook.

Write about something you did with a friend or group of friends.

Write about something new you recently learned.

Write about a problem you want to solve.

UNIT 5 REVIEW

1 **Read.** Underline the correct words.

1. A basket can be made by *embroidering / weaving* thin strips of plants.

2. A mother can *hold on / pass down* her jewelry to her children.

3. People who live here speak the *tourist / local* language.

4. A doctor is important to the *community / storytelling.*

5. My uncle is part of my father's *generation / language.*

6. I am *holding on / proud* of my cultural traditions.

7. We can hold on to the past as we build our *share / future.*

8. This is the *pottery / jewelry* we use for dinner.

2 **Listen.** Check T for *True* and F for *False.* TR: 5.5

1. (T) (F)   3. (T) (F)   5. (T) (F)   7. (T) (F)
2. (T) (F)   4. (T) (F)   6. (T) (F)   8. (T) (F)

3 **Ask and answer.** Work with a partner. Student 1, go to the bottom of page 123 and ask a question. Student 2, go to the bottom of page 125 and look at the pictures and answer. Take turns.

What kind of handcrafted art is he making?

He is making a sculpture!

4 **Read and write the correct words.** Then listen and check your answers. TR: 5.6

1. (*Hit / Kick*) _____ the TV with your hand won't turn it on!

2. I'm interested in (*read / watch*) _____ the ball game.

3. Have you tried (*lift / push*) _____ the green button?

4. No. Do you think (*try / write*) _____ that button will start the TV?

5. Of course! I always turn it on by (*run / use*) _____ the green button.

6. You were right! My TV turns on by (*touch / scratch*) _____ the bottom of the screen.

7. Your TV is newer, but I like (*show / learn*) _____ people how this TV works.

8. Thanks for (*help / know*) _____ me!

5 **Read and write.** Choose the best word to complete the sentences correctly.

1. _____Telling_____ stories is hard to do well. I like _____listening_____ to stories! (*listen / tell*)

2. _____ soup on cold days can keep you warm. I also think _____ on a sweater can help you keep warm. (*put / eat*)

3. I heard you _____ with Paula. She likes _____ jokes. (*laugh / tell*)

4. _____ is the best way to stay healthy. I like _____ to the pool. (*go / swim*)

5. _____ baseball taught me how to catch a ball. _____ the ball is much harder. (*hit / play*)

6. _____ your culture keeps it alive for the next generation. I think that _____ about culture is important. (*learn / pass down*)

6 **Read and write.** Write sentences about what you like or enjoy.

1. Playing the guitar is fun! I enjoy playing the guitar with my brother. _____

2. _____

3. _____

4. _____

5. _____

Unit 6
Amazing Plants!

VOCABULARY 1

 Read and write. Do the puzzle.

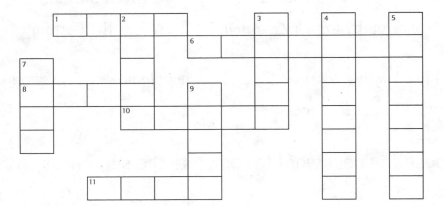

adapt	nutrients
attract	root
bacteria	stem
behavior	stink
insects	strategy
leaf	trap
light	trick

Across

1. After it turned brown, I picked the biggest ____ off the tree.

6. to draw interest

8. The scientist tried to ____ the animal that escaped.

10. How could that be true? It must be a(n) ____!

11. part of a plant that grows down into the ground

Down

2. The animals had to ____ to the sudden change in temperature.

3. to smell bad

4. tiny creatures that change nutrients into food

5. a plan or way to do something

7. Be careful! The ____ of that rose has many sharp thorns.

9. Plants need ____ from the sun to grow.

2 Complete the sentences.

adapt   attract   behavior   digest

1. The smell of rotting meat will _____ some flies.

2. Some plants can _____ meat to get their nutrition.

3. Plants must _____ to the places where they grow.

4. The _____ of bees includes carrying pollen from flower to flower.

3 Label the picture. Match the words to the picture.

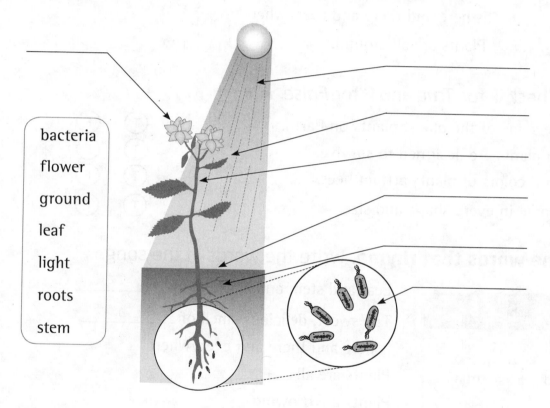

bacteria
flower
ground
leaf
light
roots
stem

4 Complete the sentences. Choose a word pair that correctly completes each sentence.

leaves / light

stinks / trick

strategy / trap

survival / digest

1. The _____ of some plants is to attract and _____ insects.

2. A plant that _____ like rotting meat can _____ flies.

3. The _____ of a plant take in _____ from the sun.

4. A _____ strategy of some plants is to _____ meat.

SONG

1 **Listen. Complete each line to finish the song.** TR: 6.1

grow
root
smell
stem
surprise
survive
sweet
tricks

Some plants play _____ with our eyes.
They're made to give us a _____.
A plant is designed to _____.
To make new seeds, to _____ and thrive.

Leaf and _____ and flower and _____!
The _____, delicious _____ of fruit
is here and there and everywhere!
Plants are all around.

2 **Listen. Check T for *True* and F for *False*.** TR: 6.2

1. Trees are some of the oldest plants on Earth. Ⓣ Ⓕ
2. Only big plants are designed to survive. Ⓣ Ⓕ
3. The bright colors of plants attract bees. Ⓣ Ⓕ
4. Plants come in every shape and size. Ⓣ Ⓕ

3 **Match the words that rhyme.** Write the words in the song.

A	B
root	all
around	fruit
size	eyes
small	down

Leaf and stem and flower and _____!
The sweet, delicious smell of _____
is here and there and everywhere!
Plants are all _____.
Plants are growing
up and _____.
Air is flowing
all around.
Plants come in every shape and _____.
Their bright colors attract the _____
of bees and butterflies.
Big and _____,
plants survive it _____.

GRAMMAR 1

1 **Read.** Complete the sentences.

1. Some plants (cook) _____are cooked_____ for food.

2. Flowers and leaves (eat) _____ by different insects.

3. The butterfly (attract) _____ to colorful flowers.

4. The pollen (carry) _____ on the legs of insects.

2 **Read and complete.** Use the words in parentheses to complete the paragraph.

Cacti plants (*find*) ____are found____ in the desert. Water (*store*) _____ in the large stem of the cactus. Any rainwater that falls (*absorb*) _____ in the roots. Cacti (*grow*) _____ in home gardens and (*plant*) _____ in desert parks. Cacti have sharp spines. Be careful, don't touch them!

3 **Read and write**. Rewrite the sentences.

1. The sun fills the room with light.
_____*The room is filled with light*_____ from the sun.

2. Leaves cover the stem of the plant.
_____ with leaves.

3. The smell of the plant attracts bees.
_____ to the smell of the plant.

4. The leaf traps the insect.
_____ by the leaf.

VOCABULARY 2

1 Read and write.

1. The white petals of a _____ are long and flat.

2. The stems of most roses have _____ that hurt.

3. I'm using colorful, dry _____ in an art project.

4. One kind of rose has _____ that climb.

5. _____ are famous for their smell.

daisy

petals

roses

thorns

vines

2 Listen and answer the questions. TR: 6.3

1. What kind of rose has small flowers?

_____

2. What kind of flower has thorns? Where are the thorns located?

_____

3. What kind of smell do most roses have?

_____

4. Where do daisies come from?

_____

5. Where can you find daisies now?

_____

6. What is the yellow center of the daisy?

_____

A climbing rose

A daisy

3 Check T for *True* and F for *False*.

1. Daisies do not have thorns.   (T)   (F)

2. The center of a daisy is often yellow.   (T)   (F)

3. Some roses stand up on strong stems.   (T)   (F)

4. Most roses don't have thorns.   (T)   (F)

GRAMMAR 2

Relative clauses with *that*

I have a <u>plant</u>.	<u>It</u> kills insects.

I have a plant **that** kills insects.

A rose has <u>thorns</u>.	<u>They</u> can hurt you.

A rose has thorns **that** can hurt you.

The Amazon is a <u>rain forest</u>.	<u>It</u> is in South America.

The Amazon is a rain forest **that** is in South America.

Botanists are <u>scientists</u>.	<u>They</u> study plants.

Botanists are scientists **that** study plants.

that or *which* = things *I have a plant <u>that / which</u> kills insects.*
that or *who* = people *Botanists are scientists <u>that / who</u> study plants.*

1 **Listen and match.** TR: 6.4

1. I see some trees	a. that grow in a garden.
2. I see some roses	b. that stand up in the sun.
3. I see some daisies	c. that live under a tree.
4. I see some leaves	d. that live in the ground!
5. I see some flowers	e. that fall on the ground.
6. I can't see bacteria	f. that move in the wind.

2 **Write sentences.** Make two sentences into one sentence.

1. The ground has nutrients. Nutrients turn into food.
   <u>The ground has nutrients that turn into food.</u>

2. Some plants digest flies. Flies are trapped on the leaves of some plants.

   _____

3. Most roses have strong stems. Most rose stems are covered with thorns.

   _____

4. Some plants have a stink. A stink attracts flies.

   _____

5. Some roses grow on vines. Vines climb up trees.

   _____

1 Listen and read. TR: 6.5

The Flypaper Plant

The butterwort is a plant that needs meat! Most species grow in wet areas of Central and South America. Butterworts can't get enough nutrients from the ground. What do they do? Insects are added as a food!

The flower of the butterwort is purple. It sits on a tall stem that has no leaves. All the leaves are near the ground. They are bright green with turned-up edges. The top of the leaf is shiny and watery. Thirsty insects are tricked by the watery leaf. It isn't water! Instead, it's a sticky water that feels like butter!

When an insect lands on a leaf, it is trapped. The insect is stuck on the leaf like a fly on flypaper. When it tries to get away, the butterwort makes more sticky water. The edges of the leaf turn up even more to hold the sticky water. Slowly, the soft parts of the insect are digested by the sticky water. It's a strategy for survival that works! Butterwort leaves often have spots that are really tiny insect skeletons!

2 **Check T for *True* and F for *False*.**

1. Most butterwort species grow in dry areas of Central and South America.   (T)   (F)

2. The butterwort grows in ground that has lots of nutrients.   (T)   (F)

3. The leaves of the butterwort are high on the stem.   (T)   (F)

4. Insects are digested by a sticky water on the leaves.   (T)   (F)

3 Label the picture. Use information from Activity 1.

bright green

purple

sticky

stuck

tall

turned-up

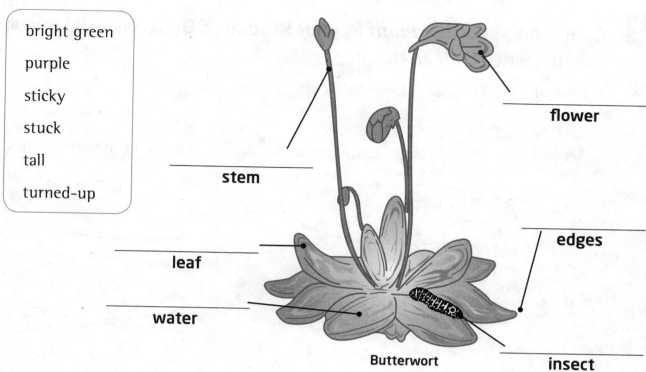

stem

flower

leaf

edges

water

Butterwort

insect

4 Read and write. Number the order of events that happen when a fly is trapped.

◯ The insect gets stuck on the leaf like a fly on flypaper.

◯ The soft parts of the insect are digested.

◯ More sticky fluid is made, and the edges of the leaf turn up.

◯ The insect flies onto the leaf.

5 Write. Describe as many parts of the butterwort plant as you can. Then compare your answers with a partner.

The stem _____ has no leaves _____.

The stem _____.

The leaves _____.

The leaves _____.

The top of the leaf _____.

_____

_____

WRITING

1 **Read _The Sensitive Plant_ in your Student's Book.** How did the writer plan the writing? Read the steps below.

1. First, the writer chose a topic. What was the writer's topic?

   _____

2. Second, the writer wrote descriptions of the details. What are the parts of the plant?

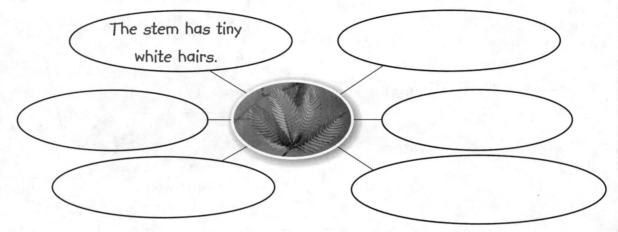

The stem has tiny white hairs.

3. Third, the writer wrote about actions. What does the plant do?

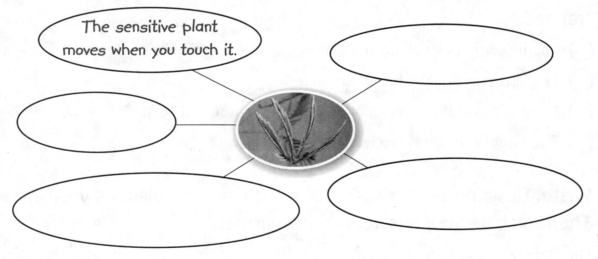

The sensitive plant moves when you touch it.

4. Fourth, the writer wrote an introduction.

   Did you know that some plants can move? The sensitive plant moves when you touch it.

5. Fifth, the writer wrote a conclusion.

   After a half hour, the plant stands up—until you touch it again!

6. Finally, the writer organized the sentences in a draft, or a first version, of the writing.

2 **Write a description.** Look at Activity 2 in your Student's Book. Invent a new plant that has interesting features. What will you name it? _____

3 **Follow steps 2–6 in Activity 1.** Use the diagram below to plan your writing. Write in your notebook.

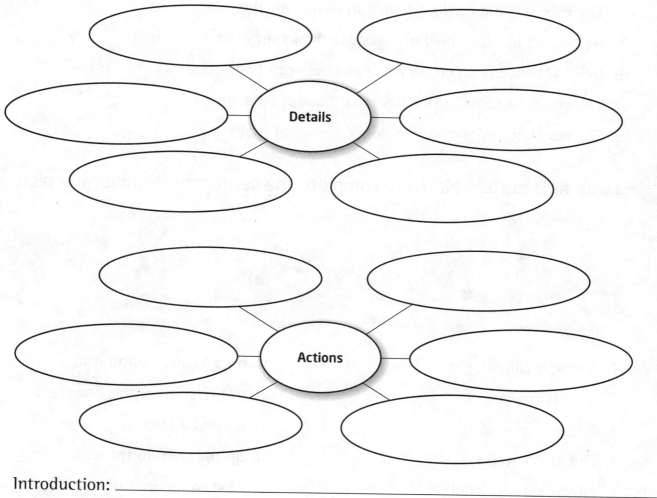

Introduction: _____

Conclusion: _____

4 **Write.** Choose one of the topics below, and write a descriptive paragraph. Plan your writing, and follow the steps in Activity 1. Write in your notebook.

Write about an amazing plant or animal.

Write about an amazing toy or tool.

Write about an amazing invention.

UNIT 6 REVIEW

1 **Read.** Underline the correct words.

1. The *roots / stems* of a tree are under the ground.

2. The *behavior / survival* of the bee is to bring pollen to other flowers.

3. My *survival / strategy* is to wait inside until the rain stops.

4. The cactus is *digested / adapted* to desert weather.

5. He doesn't like the smell of roses. He thinks they *thorns / stink*!

6. Help! My shoe is *attracted / trapped* between two rocks!

7. The colors of some butterflies *trick / adapt* predators.

8. She hurt her finger on the *petals / thorns* of that rose!

2 **Look and match.** Match to complete the sentences. Number the pictures.

1. A vine is climbing   a. on a Venus flytrap leaf.

2. A fly is trapped   b. to the smell of the flowers.

3. A flower grows   c. around a tree.

4. The insect walks   d. up the stem to the leaf.

5. The bee is attracted   e. next to the root of a tree.

3 **Write your own sentences.** Use words you did not underline in Activity 1.

_____

_____

_____

_____

_____

4 **Read and match.** Draw lines to connect the two parts that form one sentence.

1. The pollen that sticks to bees   a. that attracts flies.

2. Rainwater is absorbed   b. in the roots of plants.

3. I like plants that   c. when it lands on a sticky leaf.

4. An insect is trapped   d. helps plants survive.

5. Rotten meat is a smell   e. is carried to other flowers.

6. Bacteria make food that   f. smell sweet to survive.

5 **Complete the sentences.** Use the words with each picture.

1.   2.   3.   4.

covered/daisies   cut/scissors   hidden/leaf   flying/flower

1. He has a garden that _____ is covered with daisies _____.

2. She smells the rose that _____.

3. He finds an insect that _____.

4. She watches the bee that _____.

6 **Read and write.** Write sentences about what you know or like about plants. Use some words from the box.

> attracted   daisy   petal   plant   rose   strategy   survival   thorn   trapped

1. I know that bees are attracted to some flowers. I like roses that grow on vines.

2. _____

3. _____

4. _____

5. _____

Review: Units 4–6

1 **Do the puzzle.** Complete the sentences. Write the first letter of each word of the answer in the puzzle. Find the hidden message!

1	2	3
Y		

4	5	6

7	8	9	10	11	
					!

1. The center of a daisy and the sun are both __Y__ __e__ __l__ __l__ __o__ __w__.

2. Earth moves on a path called an ____ ____ ____ ____ ____ around the sun.

3. There are many galaxies in the ____ ____ ____ ____ ____ ____ ____ ____.

4. Someone who leaves Earth to travel in space is called an

   ____ ____ ____ ____ ____ ____ ____ ____ ____.

5. The part of a plant that grows under the ground and gets food is the

   ____ ____ ____ ____.

6. A creature that lives on a planet that is not Earth is an ____ ____ ____ ____ ____-

   ____ ____ ____ ____ ____ ____ ____ ____ ____ ____ ____.

7. People the same age are from the same

   ____ ____ ____ ____ ____ ____ ____ ____ ____ ____.

8. A spacecraft is pushed into space by a ____ ____ ____ ____ ____ ____.

9. Making a design by sewing with colors is called

   ____ ____ ____ ____ ____ ____ ____ ____ ____ ____.

10. The air that surrounds a planet is called the

    ____ ____ ____ ____ ____ ____ ____ ____ ____ ____.

11. Someone on vacation who visits a place is called a

    ____ ____ ____ ____ ____ ____ ____.

2 Look and write. Use a word pair to write a sentence for each picture.

insect/petal   leaf/trapped   roots/ground   rose/thorns   stem/daisy   vine/holding on

_____

_____

3 Read and write. Complete the sentences.

1. A spacecraft _____is carried_____ (*carry*) by a rocket.

2. Our traditions _____ (*share*) by the whole family.

3. The future of space travel _____ (*debate*) by scientists.

4. Two languages _____ (*speak*) by the local people.

5. Mars _____ (*orbit*) by two moons.

6. The shirt _____ (*embroider*) with colorful stripes.

4 Listen. Check T for *True* or F for *False*. TR: 6.6

1. Recordings of TV shows are included on the records.　　Ⓣ　　Ⓕ

2. Knowing about Earth might interest extraterrestrials.　　Ⓣ　　Ⓕ

3. The records include examples of many languages.　　Ⓣ　　Ⓕ

4. Scientists hope the records are found by extraterrestrials.　　Ⓣ　　Ⓕ

5. The *Voyager* spacecraft are orbiting Earth.　　Ⓣ　　Ⓕ

5 **Write.** Complete the sentences.

1. Storytelling is a tradition that <u>is passed down by each generation</u>. (*pass down/ generation*)

2. We live in a community that _____. (*proud/culture*)

3. Extraterrestrial life is a topic that _____. (*debate/scientists*)

4. Astronauts live in a space station that _____. (*orbit/ planet*)

5. Eating insects is a strategy that _____. (*use/plants*)

6. Plants need light that _____. (*come/sun*)

6 **Listen and write.** Complete the sentences. **TR: 6.7**

1. If handcrafted jewelry is pretty, _____ will buy it.

2. Sculpting with clay can be learned by _____.

3. Pottery can be found in _____ home.

4. Without practice, _____ can make jewelry.

7 **Read and write.** Use the words to complete each sentence.

digest   proud   stink   strategy

1. Everyone <u>should be proud</u> of their culture.

2. A plant might use _____ to attract flies.

3. Some plants _____ that are trapped in their leaves.

4. Making handcrafted art is a _____ tourists to a local community.

8 **Write.** Use at least one of the words in each sentence.

anyone   everyone   may   might   no one   someone

1. <u>There might *be someone who speaks that language*.</u>

2. _____

3. _____

4. _____

5. _____

9 **Read the text.** Choose the right words and write them on the lines.

The Amazing Cactus

Many animals can _____survive_____ in a hot and dry desert. They may use a cactus for food, water, and a home. It doesn't often rain in a desert, but the cactus saves

1 the water _____ falls on the ground. A woodpecker might be found in

2 a cactus. _____ a hole with its beak, it may make a home. When the

3 woodpecker moves away, an elf owl _____ move into the hole. The owl isn't good at digging holes, but it likes the safety that the cactus gives.

4 _____ in the cactus isn't the only way animals survive. A jackrabbit might

5 eat part of the cactus to get water. The fruit of the cactus is _____ by

6 some bats. The cactus is an amazing _____! It is part of the survival

7 _____ of many desert animals!

Example	hold on	trick	survive
1	what	who	that
2	Digging	Dig	Make
3	is	likes	may
4	Live	Living	Life
5	eaten	ate	eat
6	flower	plant	insect
7	culture	strategy	tradition

10 **Write.** Answer the questions.

1. How does the cactus help desert animals survive?

_____

2. How might a woodpecker use a cactus?

_____

3. Why would a jackrabbit eat a cactus?

_____

4. Why might an owl sometimes live in a cactus?

_____

11 **Write in your notebook.** Tell the story of a day in the life of a cactus. Write the story in your notebook.

Unit 7

Volcanoes

VOCABULARY 1

1 **Do the puzzle.** Read the clues. Fill in the words.

ash	gases
calm	heat
cover	inside
cracks	melted
creates	steam
deep	surface
erupts	thick
explodes	volcano

Across

1. A book with many pages is a ____ book.

4. When the sea has no waves, it is ____.

5. Only ____ remains after a fire burns completely.

7. Magma is melted rock ____ inside the volcano.

8. When something rises to the top of a pool of water, it rises to the ____.

10. When something breaks up and throws pieces into the air with a loud noise, it ____.

12. When something falls, it could get ____ on its surface.

15. An artist paints a painting. He ____ a work of art.

16. After the sun came out, all of the snow ____ and turned into water.

Down

2. The door of a house lets you go from the ____ to the outside.

3. It is hard to breathe near an erupting volcano because of the ____.

6. When a volcano ____, lava flows down the sides.

9. A ____ is a mountain that contains hot magma.

11. Water that is very hot turns to ____.

13. After an eruption, ash may ____ the area around a volcano.

14. ____ from the sun travels to Earth and warms us all.

2 **Write.** Complete each sentence so that it matches the picture above it.

creates   erupts   inside

The volcano _____.

The insect is _____ the jar.

She _____ a sculpture.

3 **Listen.** Check T for *True* and F for *False*. TR: 7.1

1. Geysers don't erupt.   T   F

2. Steam erupts from cracks on the surface
   of the ground.   T   F

3. The water deep inside the ground is cold.   T   F

4. The surface is covered in thick, white ash.   T   F

5. The girl likes calm vacations.   T   F

4 **Write.** What can you say? Write a sentence.

1. steam / creates / thick   The steam creates a thick, white cloud.

2. surface / covered / ash   _____

3. gases / explode / volcano   _____

4. cracks / erupt / inside   _____

5. heat / melts / deep   _____

SONG

1 **Listen to the song.** Match the phrases that are sung together. **TR: 7.2**

1. Deep inside a volcano,

2. If they have no place to go,

3. If a volcano is dormant,

4. A dormant volcano

5. If a volcano is active,

a. it's really just asleep.

b. will sleep for centuries.

c. the volcano will erupt!

d. heat and gas are building up.

e. it's very wide awake.

2 **Read and match.** Write a complete sentence from Activity 1 that describes each picture.

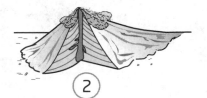
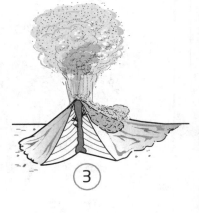

①

②

③

_____
_____
_____
_____

_____
_____
_____
_____

_____
_____
_____
_____

3 **Listen and write.** How are volcanoes like people? Complete the sentences. Then write a new verse comparing a volcano to a person. **TR: 7.3**

1. Volcanoes are a lot like me. Some are _____ and _____.

2. Other volcanoes are _____. Yes, volcanoes are a lot _____.

3. When I get really _____, and my energy builds up, if it has no place to go, sometimes I think I will _____!

_____

_____

_____

_____

GRAMMAR 1

First conditional

If	the bell	**rings,**	everyone	**will go**	inside.	
	the volcano	**erupts,**	we	**won't have**	school tomorrow.	*won't = will not*

These two sentences mean the same thing. In sentence 1, notice the comma.
If the bell rings, everyone will go inside.
Everyone will go inside if the bell rings.

1 **Read and write.** Combine the two sentences into one sentence.

1. The magma explodes. / Melted rock comes to the surface.
   <u>If the magma explodes, melted rock will come to the surface.</u>

2. The ash is hot. / It burns everything it touches.
   _____

3. Animals run away. / A volcano explodes.
   _____

4. The scientist visits a volcano. / She climbs to the top.
   _____

5. The people living near the volcano are safe. / The volcano is calm.
   _____

2 **Write.** What about you? Write sentences that say what you will do.

1. If it rains tomorrow, <u>I will bring an umbrella</u>.

2. If my pencil breaks, _____.

3. If I go to the park this weekend, _____.

4. If I like this book, _____.

5. If you come to my house, _____.

6. If you win the game, _____.

7. If I wake up early on Saturday, _____.

8. If you have a birthday party, _____.

85

VOCABULARY 2

1 **Read and look.** Match each sentence to one of the pictures.

1. This animal is dormant in winter.

2. This animal is active.

3. This animal is extinct.

2 **Read and write.** Complete each of the following sentences.

active   cone   crater   dormant   extinct

1. A(n) _____ volcano sends steam into the air.

2. When a volcano erupts, it can leave a _____ at the top.

3. Some trees are _____ in the winter and have no leaves.

4. When no animals of a species are alive, that species is _____.

5. Volcanoes are often shaped like a _____.

3 **Complete the table.** Write each phrase in the correct row.

Active	
Dormant	
Extinct	

riding a bicycle

every dinosaur

a volcano not erupting

a language no one speaks

playing football

a volcano that will never erupt

swimming in a pool

sleeping all winter

GRAMMAR 2

Because of...

There was no school		the volcano.
Airplanes could not fly	**because of**	the ash.
The trees died		the heat.

You can also say: **Because of** the volcano, there was no school. Notice the comma.

1 **Look and write.** Write about the pictures.

bike / snow	cold / open window	music / sleep
cat / barking	hot sun / water	~~rain / umbrella~~

1. Because of the rain, she had an umbrella.

2. _____

3. _____

4. _____

5. _____

6. _____

1 **Listen and read.** TR: 7.4

Eruptions That Changed the World!

Volcanoes have changed the world several times in the past. They've made cities and people disappear, and they've changed the climate for years. Have you heard of the Lost City of Atlantis? Some people think it was lost because of a volcanic eruption in Greece.

The island of Santorini (once called Thera), in Greece, is on half a volcano. The other half of the volcano exploded and disappeared in 1600 BCE. A culture, the Minoans, may have disappeared with it. Ash from the eruption has been found as far away as Egypt. Because of the explosion, crops died and rain and temperature changed for years.

Today, over two million people live near Mount Vesuvius in Italy. However, in 79 CE, it erupted. The explosion sent ash 24,000 meters (15 miles) into the air. The sky was dark because of the eruption. Hot ash ran down the cone and burned everything in its way. In two hours, two cities were gone.

Two eruptions in Indonesia changed the world. The first, Tambora in 1815, sent gases into the sky that circled Earth. Because of that eruption, Europe and North America had no summer in 1816. The weather changed a lot! In 1883, Krakatoa sent ash 60,000 meters (37 miles) into the sky! Earth's temperature dropped for five years. It was the biggest eruption in history. It erupted again in 2018. If there is another big eruption, where will it be?

2 **Read and write.** Complete the sentences.

1. Ash found in Egypt came from the eruption of _____.

2. The biggest eruption in history was _____.

3. Because of the eruption of _____, the sky was dark.

4. There was no summer in Europe and North America in 1816 because of

_____.

3 **Complete the chart.** Use information from the reading in Activity 1.

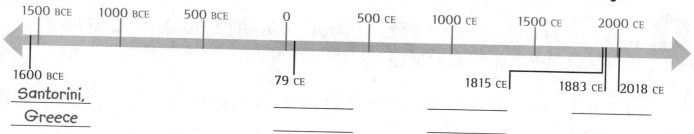

| 1500 BCE | 1000 BCE | 500 BCE | 0 | 500 CE | 1000 CE | 1500 CE | 2000 CE |

1600 BCE
Santorini,
Greece

79 CE
_____

1815 CE
_____

1883 CE
_____

2018 CE
_____

4 **Write the facts.** In the chart, list what you learned about each eruption.

Santorini (Thera)	It erupted in 1600 BCE.
Vesuvius	
Tambora	
Krakatoa	

5 **Write.** In your notebook, write three things you know about volcanoes. Then discuss with a partner.

> If a very big eruption happens again, the weather will get cooler!

> The climate can change because of volcanoes!

A floating island of rocks was found near New Zealand in 2012. It was the size of a small country! The rocks came from an underground volcano and were so light that they floated!

WRITING

1 **Read *How a Volcano Erupts* in your Student's Book.** How did the writer plan the writing? Read the steps below.

1. First, the writer chose a topic. What was the writer's topic?

   _____

2. Second, the writer wrote the series of action steps in the process.

When	Action Step
First	the chamber starts to fill with hot magma.
At the same time	hot gases fill the chamber.
When	the chamber is full, it has to escape.
Then	the volcano erupts.
Finally	the volcano calms down and it stops erupting.

3. Third, the writer used pictures to show major steps in the process.

4. Fourth, the writer wrote a summary conclusion.

   The process could start again at any moment!

5. Finally, the writer organized the sentences in a draft, or a first version, of the paragraphs.

2 **Choose a topic.** Look at Activity 2 in your Student's Book. Think of a process that you can break into steps, and describe it from beginning to end.

_____

_____

_____

_____

_____

3 **Follow steps 2-5 in Activity 1.** Use the chart and the space below to plan your ideas. Then write your process description in your notebook.

When	Action Step

Can you use pictures to show some of the major steps in the process? Describe what the pictures would show.

_____

_____

_____

_____

Draw the pictures in your notebook.

Write a summary conclusion:

_____

4 **Write.** Choose one of the topics below, and write a description of the process. Plan your writing, and follow the steps in Activity 1. Write in your notebook.

How to make your favorite snack

How to fix a broken toy or machine

How to complete a school or work task

How to do something fun or exciting

UNIT 7 REVIEW

1 **Read.** Circle the correct words.

1. A volcano is *dormant / extinct* if it has not been active for 20 years.
2. A big volcanic eruption may leave a *cone / crater* at the top of the mountain.
3. Magma can push through *deep / melted* cracks in the earth.
4. A crater is created when the cone of a volcano *covers / explodes*.
5. An eruption can release *thick / calm* clouds of steam.
6. Ash from a volcano can *erupt / cover* the land for many kilometers.
7. Gases can escape from *cones / cracks* in the *surface / cover* of the earth.
8. *Thick / Melted* rock pushes up from deep *heat / inside* a volcano.

2 **Read and write.** Choose the best two words to complete each sentence.

> calm surface   cracked surface   deep crater   heated steam   thick cover

1. Trapped gases and _____ are deep inside many volcanoes.
2. I can see my face in the _____ of the lake.
3. After it snows, the roof of my house has a _____ of snow.
4. During a heat wave, wet mud will dry and become a _____.
5. There is a lake in the _____ at the top of that dormant volcano.

3 **Write sentences.**

1. an active volcano / explode
   An active volcano can explode at any time.

2. extinct volcanoes / erupt
   _____

3. thick ash / covers
   _____

4. lava flows down / cone
   _____

5. plants are burned / heat
   _____

4 **Look and listen.** Answer the questions. Check T for *True* and F for *False*. TR: 7.5

1. Because of the ash and gases in the sky, some eruptions hide light from the sun.
2. If an eruption is small, the temperature will get cooler.
3. Salma knows about Mount Pinatubo because of her schoolwork.
4. The temperature dropped one degree Celsius because of the eruptions.
5. Scientists know about rainfall in China because of the trees they studied.

(T) (F)
(T) (F)
(T) (F)
(T) (F)
(T) (F)

5 **Read and match.** Connect the two parts to make sentences.

1. If the sky fills with gases from an eruption,
2. Because of the Mount Pinatubo eruption,
3. Scientists know it rained less in China
4. The earth's weather will change

a. because of the slower growth of the trees they studied.
b. if there is a very big volcanic eruption.
c. the earth's temperature lowered one degree Celsius.
d. it will stop some light from the sun.

6 **Work with a partner.** Student 1, go to the top of page 126 and say a sentence half. Student 2, go to the top of page 128 and say the matching sentence half. Take turns.

Because of the book I read about volcanoes,

I know about eruptions that changed Earth's weather.

Unit 8
Reduce, Reuse, Recycle

VOCABULARY 1

1 **Label the pictures.** Use the words below to complete each sentence.

| conserve | landfill | man-made | natural | recycle |
| reduce | renewable | reuse | throw away | trash |

1. Don't _____ things that you can _____.

2. You can _____ some _____ to make art.

3. It's good to use _____ products that are _____.

4. _____ stuff, such as plastics, ends up in the _____.

5. If you _____ the heating temperature, you will _____ energy.

2 Complete the sentences. Use the words below.

> build   efficient   environment   natural   trash

1. I like clothing made from cotton and other _____ materials.

2. My father bought wood to _____ a doghouse.

3. That theater uses very little electricity. It is energy _____.

4. Some people make art out of _____.

5. It's important to reduce, reuse, and recycle if we want a clean _____.

3 Listen and write. Answer the questions. TR: 8.1

1. What kind of design will the new library be?

_____

2. What is the design good for?

_____

3. What does Takuya hope about the new library?

_____

4. What will the man-made material in the walls reduce?

_____

5. What is the man-made material made from?

_____

6. What does Natsumi do with glass?

_____

7. What happens to glass that is thrown away?

_____

8. What will the city reuse from the old library?

_____

SONG

1 **Listen.** Fill in the missing words to complete the song. TR: 8.2

> recycling   reduce   reused   trash

_____. Reuse. Recycle.

Do it every day.

Don't throw everything into the _____

when clearly there's another way.

_____ is easy when you know what to do.

Glass? Paper? Metal?

These things can be _____,

again, and again, and again!

2 **Listen.** Check T for *True* and F for *False*. TR: 8.3

1. You should stop and think if trash can be reused.   T   F
2. You should do your part to keep the world green.   T   F
3. Composting is hard to do.   T   F
4. Natural things can't be reused.   T   F

3 **Listen and write.** List four things from the song that you can recycle or reuse. Then write four new lines! TR: 8.4

1. _____

2. _____

3. _____

4. _____

_____

_____

_____

_____

GRAMMAR 1

Passive with modals (simple present)

Most paper	can		recycled.	
Plastic bottles	may	be	put	in recycling.
The windows	must		closed	to save energy.

may = It's OK to do something. You have permission to do it.

1 **Read.** Complete the sentences. Use *can/may/must* and the verb in parentheses.

1. Houses _____can be built_____ (*build*) from renewable materials.

2. New cars _____ (*design*) to run more efficiently.

3. Energy _____ (*conserve*) if we turn off lights we don't need.

4. If you can't reuse or recycle a plastic, it _____ (*throw away*) in the trash.

5. The use of landfills _____ (*reduce*) by recycling more things.

6. Junk _____ (*reuse*) for other things.

7. The environment _____ (*make*) more beautiful.

8. Some man-made materials _____ (*recycle*).

2 **Complete the paragraph.**

> grow   make   recycle   use   wash

We use too many man-made materials. Natural materials _____ more often. They are renewable and often _____ on farms.

For example, clothing _____ from cotton. Cotton is strong, and it feels good to wear. When it gets dirty, it _____. When it is too old, it

_____. It is a useful and practical natural material!

VOCABULARY 2

1 **Read and look.** Match each word to one of the pictures.

> cardboard glass tools
> chemicals metal

1. Don't pour dangerous _____ down the sink!

2. Use the right _____ to put up a picture.

3. Use a can opener to open a _____ can.

4. Windows are made of _____.

5. Store things in a _____ box.

2 **Read and match.**

1. Glass can be used
2. Metal can be made
3. Tools can be designed
4. Chemicals must be kept
5. Cardboard may be cut

a. into chains and jewelry.
b. in closed bottles or cans.
c. to make bottles.
d. with scissors.
e. to make work easier.

3 **Write.** What can be used? Use words from Activity 1.

This material can be used to make . . .

1. boxes and paper plates: _____

2. cleaning products, medicines, batteries, and toothpaste: _____

3. bottles, windows, jars, and light bulbs: _____

4. cans, cars, pots, and bikes: _____

GRAMMAR 2

Clauses with *when*

| When | you reuse paper bags, | you save trees. |
| | I finish drinking water, | I recycle the bottle. |

These two sentences mean the same thing. In sentence 1, notice the comma.
When you reuse paper bags, you save trees.
You save trees when you reuse paper bags.

1 **Look and write.** Write about each picture.

> use a glass bottle   ~~buy natural things~~   turn off a light
>
> pick up trash from the ground   build a compost bin

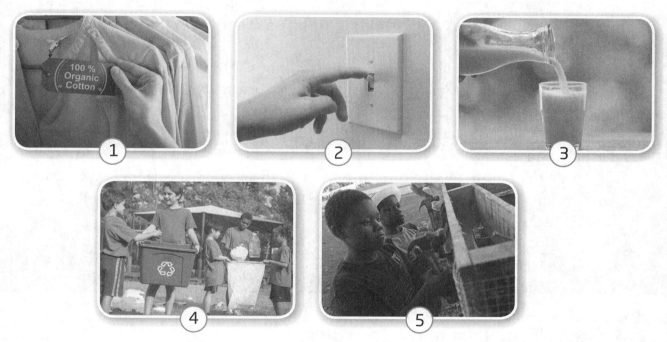

1. When we buy natural things, _____ we are buying renewable materials.

2. We conserve electricity _____.

3. We may be using recycled glass _____.

4. _____ we make the environment cleaner.

5. We use a tool _____.

1 **Listen and read.** TR: 8.5

E-waste Recycling

What do we do with broken TVs, computers, phones, and electronic parts? They become e-waste, or electronic waste. Most e-waste is thrown away in landfills. However, e-waste can be recycled.

Electronic parts have useful metals in them. Energy is used when the parts are recycled to get the metal. But even more energy is needed to get new metal from rocks. So recycling metal uses less energy. It only takes 5 percent of the energy to recycle the metal in some cans.

Metals and chemicals must be removed from e-waste to protect the environment. The chemicals in e-waste can be bad for the water and the earth. Some e-waste has chemicals to stop fires. These chemicals can harm babies. Electronic parts often have dangerous metals. If these metals turn into chemicals in water, they are bad for people.

E-waste often has plastic in it. When we burn plastic, it lets off poisonous gases. When we recycle plastic, it is safer. It takes a lot of energy to make new plastic. Recycling plastic uses only about 70 percent of the energy. When we make electronics, we also make gases that hurt the atmosphere. We reduce the amount of those gases when we recycle.

It's important to recycle e-waste and not throw it away in a landfill. We must also try to make electronic parts that use safer materials. Recycling is good, but reducing is better!

2 **Check T for *True* and F for *False*.**

1. Most e-waste is recycled. Ⓣ Ⓕ

2. Less energy is needed to recycle cans than to make them. Ⓣ Ⓕ

3. Electronics often have dangerous metals in them. Ⓣ Ⓕ

4. Chemicals in e-waste can harm people. Ⓣ Ⓕ

5. The plastic in e-waste must be burned. Ⓣ Ⓕ

6. Electronics must be made with safer materials. Ⓣ Ⓕ

3 **Complete the chart.** Use information from the reading in Activity 1.

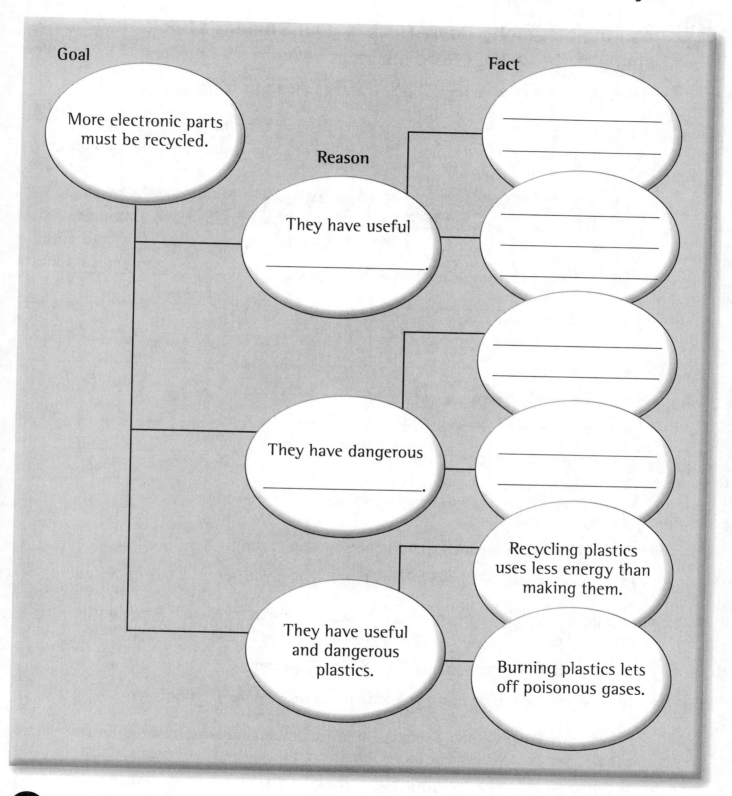

Goal

More electronic parts must be recycled.

Reason

They have useful

_____.

They have dangerous

_____.

They have useful and dangerous plastics.

Fact

_____
_____

_____
_____
_____

_____
_____

_____
_____

Recycling plastics uses less energy than making them.

Burning plastics lets off poisonous gases.

4 **Write.** Rank the importance of the three reasons from Activity 3. Write a sentence to explain your ranking in your notebook.

WRITING

1 **Read the biography** *David Mach* **in your Student's Book.** How did the writer plan the writing? Read the steps below.

1. First, the writer chose a topic. What was the writer's topic?

_____

2. Second, the writer wrote important dates, events, and facts. Complete the notes.

Key Dates	Important Events	Interesting Facts
He was born in Scotland in 1956.	His first exhibition was in London.	Some of his sculptures are made of metal coat hangers.

3. Third, the writer explained why the person is important.

   He is famous for his big sculptures that use many different kinds of objects.

4. Fourth, the writer used expressions that show importance, such as *famous, around the world, most famous,* and *huge.*

   He is an artist and is famous for his big sculptures.

   He has now had exhibitions in many cities around the world.

5. Finally, the writer wrote a sentence of introduction and organized the sentences into a draft, or a first version, of the biography.

   David Mach was born in Scotland in 1956.

2 **Write a biography.** See Activity 2 in your Student's Book. First, choose a topic for your writing.

_____

3 **Follow steps 2-5 in Activity 1.** Use the chart and the space below to plan. Then write your biography in your notebook.

Key Dates	Important Events	Interesting Facts

Write why the person is important:

_____

Write expressions that show importance:

_____

4 **Write.** Choose one of the topics below and write a biography. Plan your writing and follow the steps in Activity 1. Write in your notebook.

Write about someone famous in your country.
Write about a successful athlete.
Write about a person who is important in your life.

UNIT 8 REVIEW

1 **Read.** Circle the correct words.

1. Batteries can be *recycled / conserved* after they stop working.

2. Plastic is a *natural / man-made* material.

3. Recycled *glass / metal* can be used to make bike parts.

4. A TV left out in the rain becomes *junk / metal*.

5. We must all *reduce / reuse* our use of energy.

6. Things that are sent to a *cardboard / landfill* become *chemicals / trash*.

7. We must *reduce / build* cars that are more *energy efficient / natural*.

8. It's bad for the *trash / environment* to put *chemicals / tools* directly in a landfill.

2 **Listen.** Check T for *True* and F for *False*. **TR: 8.6**

1. Sara says that plastic is a renewable material. (T) (F)

2. Adam says that some natural things can be man-made. (T) (F)

3. Sara says that plants can be used for fuel. (T) (F)

4. Sara puts a man-made chemical on her salad. (T) (F)

5. Adam says that most chemicals are not renewable. (T) (F)

6. Sara says that cooking oil can't be reused. (T) (F)

7. Adam says that oil is renewable. (T) (F)

8. Sara says that recycling oil is efficient. (T) (F)

3 **Ask and answer.** Work with a partner. Student 1, go to the bottom of page 126 and ask a question. Student 2, go to the bottom of page 128 and say the answer. Take turns asking and answering.

Why should we conserve energy?

Because it reduces the energy we need to make.

4 **Listen and write.** Complete each sentence. TR: 8.7

1. When we all help, (*environment*) _____ we can make the environment cleaner _____.

2. When we reduce, recycle, and reuse, (*teach*) _____.

3. More (*energy*) _____ when we reuse instead of recycle.

4. Our use of energy (*reduce*) _____.

5. Fernanda thinks that our use of paper (*reduce*) _____.

6. Fernanda says that both sides of a piece of paper (*use*) _____.

5 **Read and write.** Complete the sentences.

1. When we care about the environment, _____.

2. _____ can be used to _____.

3. We help keep the planet green _____.

4. _____ must be put _____.

6 **Write.** Write a sentence about how people make waste. Then write a sentence about how people can stop making so much waste.

1. When we _print things, we waste paper!_ _____

Paper can be reused or recycled. _____

2. _____

_____

3. _____

_____

4. _____

_____

Unit 9
Cool Vacations!

VOCABULARY 1

1 **Look and write.** Use the words below to complete the sentences for each photo.

> beach   camping   guide   hike   hotel   photo safari   relax
>
> ruins   tent   theme park   tickets   tour   water park   wildlife

1. You can _____ by the
   pool at the _____.

2. They are _____. They
   are sitting in a _____.

3. They are going for a _____.
   The person at the front is the
   _____.

4. They are buying _____
   for a _____.

5. They are taking a _____
   of the _____.

6. They can see _____ on
   a _____.

7. They are running on the _____.

8. He is playing at a _____.

2 **Rank the vacations.** Write a sentence to say why you want to go on each one.

> on a photo safari   see ruins   to a theme park   to a water park

1. First, I want to go _____ because _____

   _____.

2. Second, I want to go _____ because _____

   _____.

3. Third, I want to go _____ because _____

   _____.

4. Fourth, I want to go _____ because _____

   _____.

SONG

1 **Listen to the song.** Fill in the missing words to complete the song. **TR: 9.1**

> beach   camping   hiking   hotel   photos
> relax   tour   vacation   wildlife

If we went on a _____,
we would see _____.
I would take lots of _____.
Wouldn't that be so nice?

I would like to stay at a _____.
You'd like to _____.

_____ and _____!
The _____ and the sun!
If we went on _____,
it would be so much fun!

2 **Connect the words that rhyme.** Circle the words. Connect the rhyming words with lines. Then listen to the song to check your answers. **TR: 9.2**

Let's go on vacation!
Let's go on a trip!

If we went on vacation,
we would take a big, big ship.
across the ocean,
far, far away.

If I had my way,
I would go today!

If I weren't afraid of heights,
we could climb a mountain.
But I am! So let's go to the water park
and take pictures by the fountain.

GRAMMAR 1

Second conditional

If								$I'd = $
	I	**lived**	near a beach,	I	**would go**	swimming every day.	$I'd = $ I would
	he	**had**	money,	he	**would buy**	a new bike.	
	I	**were**	rich,	I	**'d travel**	around the world.	he'd =
	he	**didn't have**	homework,	he	**'d play**	video games.	he would

Real situation: *I don't live near the beach, so I can't go swimming every day.*
Imagined situation: *If I **lived** near a beach, I **would go** swimming every day.*
With *were*: *If I/you/he/she/we/they **were** rich . . .*

1 Read and underline the answer.

I like to take photos when I'm on vacation. If I *went / would go* on a photo safari,
I *took / would take* photos of zebras. If we *saw / would see* lions, I *don't want /
would not want* to get too close. If the lions *came / would come* near the car, I *was /
would be* afraid. I *liked / would like* it better if they *were / would be* giraffes. Giraffes have
long necks and tongues. If I *saw / would see* a giraffe, I *took / would take* lots of photos.
I *showed / would show* the photos to you if you *came / would come* to my house. If you
wanted / would want to take one home with you, I *was / would be* happy to give one to you!

2 Read. Complete the sentences.

1. If I _____went_____ (go) on a photo safari, I ___would see___ (see) wildlife.

2. They _____ (go) to a theme park if they _____ (have) tickets.

3. He _____ (not go) to the beach if he _____ (have) homework.

4. She _____ (have) a guide with her if she _____ (go) on a tour.

5. I _____ (visit) the ruins if I _____ (go) to Egypt.

3 Read and write. Complete the sentences.

1. If the water park were open, _____. (buy)

2. I would sleep outside _____. (have)

3. If you liked wildlife, _____. (go)

4. She would take a ship _____. (go)

5. If I went to the beach, _____. (swim)

6. He would be a guide _____. (know)

VOCABULARY 2

1 **Look and label.**

_____   _____   _____   _____   _____

2 **Read and write.** Use the words from Activity 1.

1. My mom wears _____ when it is a sunny day outside.

2. The screen at the _____ showed the time that planes would arrive.

3. My brother has a _____ with wheels to make it easy to carry.

4. My sister bought a _____ so that she would remember our vacation.

5. My dad showed his _____ at the airport when we returned to our country.

3 **Listen and answer the questions.** TR: 9.3

1. Where did Aunt Frida take the family?

_____

2. What did Rosa's dad show at the airport?

_____

3. What did Rosa get on vacation?

_____

4. What did Julio get on vacation?

_____

5. What did Julio think he left on vacation?

_____

6. What was Rosa's surprise for Julio?

_____

GRAMMAR 2

Would rather

I'd rather	watch a movie	than	play a video game.	I'd = I would
He'd rather	go swimming		(go) hiking.	He'd = He would

Question				Answer
Would you rather	go on a trip	or	stay home?	I'd rather go on a trip.
Would he rather	visit England		(visit) Australia?	He'd rather visit Australia.

When the verbs are the same, we don't usually say the second verb.
I'd rather go swimming than hiking.
Would he rather visit England or Australia?

1 Read and write.

1. I / go to the movies / go to a baseball game
   I would rather go to the movies than (go) to a baseball game.

2. He / dance to hip-hop / dance to rock and roll
   _____

3. They / go swimming in a pool / go swimming in a lake
   _____

4. We / visit a museum / go to a concert
   _____

2 Complete the sentences.

1. She _'d rather eat breakfast than go to school hungry_____. (breakfast / hungry)
2. They _____. (home / vacation)
3. She _____. (city / small town)
4. He _____. (music / movie)

3 Write. Rewrite your answers to Activity 2 as questions.

1. _Would she rather eat breakfast or go to school hungry?_
2. _____
3. _____
4. _____

1 Listen and read. TR: 9.4

The Forbidden City

It's weird but true! A city was built 600 years ago for one family! The Forbidden City in Beijing, China, was built for the emperor of China. No one could enter the city without the emperor's invitation.

Building on the Forbidden City started in 1406. It was completed 14 years later. For 500 years, the Forbidden City was the home of 24 emperors. Over the years, fires destroyed some buildings, but they were rebuilt each time. The main building was burned by fires in 1557 and 1597. After a battle in 1644, a bigger fire burned buildings in the city.

Today, the Forbidden City has 980 buildings on 720,000 square meters of land. The buildings are made of painted wood. The city has bridges of marble, stone statues, and brick streets. It is surrounded by a wall 10 meters high. A river of water that is 6 meters deep surrounds the wall. The walls and river protected the emperor from outsiders.

The Forbidden City was first opened to the public as a museum in 1925. In 1987, the Forbidden City was made a World Heritage Site. Today, tourists can visit many of the buildings and see some of the emperors' treasures. Millions of people visit the city that was forbidden for hundreds of years! It is an important part of Chinese history. It is also the largest collection of preserved wooden structures in the world!

2 Check T for *True* and F for *False*.

1. The Forbidden City was built for tourists.
2. The Forbidden City is the largest building in the world.
3. The Forbidden City is now a museum.
4. The Forbidden City is surrounded by a tall wall.

3 Complete the chart. Use information from the reading in Activity 1.

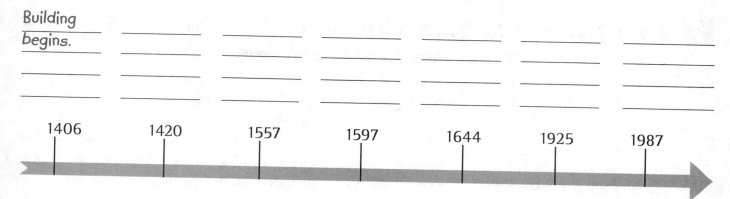

Building
begins.

1406	1420	1557	1597	1644	1925	1987

4 What did you learn? Add more information using numbers from the reading.

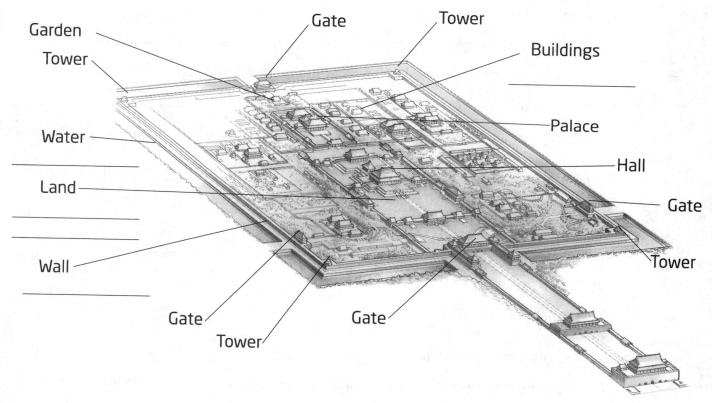

5 Write. Read the questions and write your opinions in your notebook. Then compare your opinions with a partner.

In your opinion . . .

1. Why was the city so large?

2. Why were the walls so high?

3. Why were there so many buildings?

4. Why were the walls surrounded by water?

WRITING

  Read *Review of the Antigua Ecotour* in your Student's Book.
How did the writer plan the writing? Read the steps below.

1. First, the writer chose a topic. What was the writer's topic?

   _____

2. Second, the writer wrote descriptions. What did the writer describe?

   a. The tour guide takes your group on a boat to <u>a natural rock bridge called Hell's Gate</u>.

   b. You have to swim to _____.

   c. Then you walk across _____.

   d. On the boat, the guide gives you _____.

   e. The boat stops at a coral reef, and you can _____.

   f. You can see wildlife, such as _____.

   g. When you get back to the boat, there is _____.

3. Third, the writer wrote opinions, or feelings. How did the writer like the ecotour?

   a. The view from the top <u>was spectacular</u>!

   b. The water can be rough, so snorkeling _____.

   c. It's worth _____.

   d. The banana bread was _____.

4. Fourth, the writer wrote an introduction.

   *If you wanted a special vacation on a beautiful island, where would you go?
   I recommend this ecotour in Antigua.*

5. Fifth, the writer wrote a conclusion.

   *If you prefer doing something active on vacation instead of sitting on a beach,
   this is the trip for you!*

6. Finally, the writer organized the sentences in a draft, or a first version,
   of the review.

2 **Write a review of a vacation.** See Activity 2 in your Student's Book. Choose a topic for your writing.

_____

3 **Follow steps 2-6 in Activity 1.** Use the lines below to plan. Write your paragraph in your notebook.

Write descriptions:

_____

_____

_____

Write what you liked and did not like:

_____

_____

_____

Write an introduction:

_____

Write a conclusion:

_____

4 **Write.** Choose one of the topics below and write a review. Plan your writing and follow the steps in Activity 1. Write your review in your notebook.

Write a review of a book you read.
Write a review of a movie you saw.
Write a review of an event, such as a dance, sports match, or cultural event.

UNIT 9 REVIEW

1 **Read.** Circle the correct words.

1. Let's go to the *passport / airport*.
2. She bought a *ticket / souvenir* to enter the theme park.
3. Put your clothes in the *suitcase / camping*.
4. Where is the key to the *hotel / tent* room?
5. I like to *hike / relax* at the *beach / ticket*.
6. I am wearing the same *sunglasses / passport* as the *wildlife / guide*.

2 **Look and write.** Compare the two vacations in the photos.

1. If you went on vacation to these places, what would you take with you?

   Photo 1: _____

   Photo 2: _____

2. If you went on vacation to these places, what would you do?

   Photo 1: _____

   Photo 2: _____

3. Which place would you rather visit?

   I would rather _____ because _____

   _____.

3 Listen and write. Answer the questions. TR: 9.5

1. What would the boy rather do if he saw a sandstorm?

_____

2. What would the girl do if she saw a poisonous snake?

_____

3. What would the boy rather play on the piano?

_____

4. If the girl had a spacecraft, what would she do?

_____

5. If the boy had a rose, what would he rather do?

_____

4 Read. Complete the sentences.

1. If I _____ (*see*) a souvenir I liked,

   I _____ (*buy*) it.

2. They _____ (*rather listen*) to a concert.

3. If she _____ (*have*) a dog, she

   _____ (*take*) it for a walk.

4. We _____ (*play*) basketball if we

   _____ (*have*) a ball.

5. You _____ (*rather sleep*) a little longer.

6. She _____ (*rather hike*) another

   2 kilometers (1.25 miles) than swim 5 kilometers

   (3.1 miles).

5 Play a game with your partner. Go to page 127.

Review: Units 7–9

1 **Match.** Connect the words that have opposite meanings. Then label the pictures.

1. active   a. surface

2. deep   b. ice

3. steam   c. dormant

_____   _____   _____

2 **Read.** Complete the sentences.

> build   cover   hike   reduce   relax   throw away

1. They plan to _____ the house with wood.

2. Don't _____ your ticket. We need to go back into the theme park.

3. The sun is so bright that I must wear sunglasses or _____ my eyes.

4. We would like to _____ up the mountain.

5. I'm so tired that I want to sit under a tree and _____.

6. It's cheaper to visit the theme park in winter because they _____ the price of the tickets.

3 Read and write. Complete the sentences.

1. If we recycle plastic, _____*we will help conserve energy*_____. (*conserve*)
2. If we create local art, _____. (*tourists*)
3. If I visit the ruins, _____. (*guide*)
4. If they have the tools, _____. (*build*)
5. If you go on a photo safari, _____. (*wildlife*)
6. If you eat ice cream on a hot day, _____. (*melt*)

4 Look and listen. Number the pictures. TR: 9.6

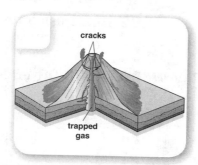

5 Read and write. Complete the sentences.

1. If the cone of an active volcano has cracks, _____*trapped gas will escape*_____. (*gas/escape*)

2. If tourist money can protect the environment, _____. (*wildlife/extinct*)

3. If a theme park is designed well, _____. (*rides/safe*)

4. If people who work at a glass factory wear special clothes, _____. (*protect/heat*)

5. If bread is cooked in a hot oven, _____. (*heat/crust*)

6. If you buy tour tickets the day before, _____. (*go/tour*)

6 Read and answer.

active volcano　buy souvenirs　go to the airport
~~recycle plastic~~　use cardboard　want to relax

1. We help keep the environment clean _____when we recycle plastic_____.

2. We may be in danger _____.

3. You must show your passport _____.

4. She can go to a resort _____.

5. _____, we can put them in our suitcases.

6. _____, I use a renewable resource.

7 Look at the three pictures. The family wants to go on vacation. Write a paragraph about their story.

_____

_____

_____

_____

_____

_____

_____

8 **Read.** Check T for *True* and F for *False*.

If you like warm weather, sandy beaches, and lots of fun things to do, you will like Dubai! Dubai is a great place to go on vacation! It is on the Arabian Peninsula. A *peninsula* is land that stretches into the water like a big toe.

Dubai is a very modern place. You can stay at a hotel on a man-made island. If you visit Dubai, you will see one of the tallest buildings in the world. It's over 800 meters (2,625 feet) tall! If you would rather go to a theme park, there are many choices. At one theme park, activities about nature, culture, science, and space can be found. You can play a game that is like flying a real airplane at this theme park.

You can also see Dubai from the air in a hot-air balloon. If you would rather ride a camel in the desert, you can! Because of the warm weather, it doesn't snow in Dubai, but you can still play in the snow inside a shopping mall. There is man-made snow and a mountain! If you would rather go in the water, a water park is nearby. There is even a park where you can swim with dolphins! If you go to Dubai, you will have a lot of fun!

1. Dubai is a modern place.   (T) (F)

2. A hotel can be found on a man-made island.   (T) (F)

3. If you went to Dubai, you would not find any theme parks.   (T) (F)

4. If you like snow, you will find it in a shopping mall in Dubai.   (T) (F)

5. You cannot ride a camel in Dubai.   (T) (F)

9 **Write.** Think about a fun place you would like to go on vacation. Would you like to take friends with you? Make a plan. Who would you invite? What would you do?

_____

_____

_____

_____

4 **Ask and answer the questions together.** Use the words in parentheses and the sentences below the questions.

1. How cold was it today? (and)

   The temperature dropped 4 degrees, and it ended up at 15 degrees.

2. Did the storm have thunder and lightning? (but)

   _____

3. What did you bring for the storm? (we)

   _____

4. Was there a storm with high winds? (with)

   _____

5. What was the range of temperatures yesterday? (and)

   _____

1. The temperature dropped 4 degrees.

2. The storm was too far away to see lightning.

3. I brought a flashlight.

4. There were very strong winds.

5. The temperature dropped to 18 degrees.

Unit 2 Student 1, use with Activity 2 on page 24.

2 **Ask and answer.** Ask each other questions about these animal adaptations.

> Why do many animals have whiskers?

> To find out if they can fit into a specific area.

Unit 4 Student 1, use with Activity 6 on page 53.

6 **Ask and answer.** Ask your partner one question. Respond to your partner's question with the correct answer from the list below. Take turns.

Questions:
1. Can everyone see the comet in the sky?
2. Can someone breathe on another planet?
3. Does no one want to take a journey to Mars?
4. Does anyone know how far Earth is from the sun?

Answers for your partner:
a. I may watch it after I finish my school work.
b. Some people say we should only think about Earth.
c. Data from intelligent life may be hidden by noise in space.
d. Maria says she wants to visit another planet.

Unit 5 Student 1, use with Activity 3 on page 64.

3 **Ask and answer.** Ask your partner a question about a picture on the left. Then respond to your partner's question with the correct answer from the right.

1.
what / embroider

a.
stripes

2.
how / show pride in local art

b.

4 **Ask and answer the questions together.** Use the words in parentheses and the sentences below the questions.

1. How cold was it today? (and)

   The temperature dropped 4 degrees, and it ended up at 15 degrees.

2. Did the storm have thunder and lightning? (but)

   _____

3. What did you bring for the storm? (we)

   _____

4. Was there a storm with high winds? (with)

   _____

5. What was the range of temperatures yesterday? (and)

   _____

1. The temperature ended up at 15 degrees.
2. There was thunder.
3. I brought supplies, including food and water.
4. There was a hurricane.
5. The temperature rose to 22 degrees.

2 **Ask and answer.** Ask each other questions about these animal adaptations.

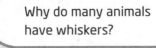

Why do many animals have whiskers?

To find out if they can fit into a specific area.

Unit 4 Student 2, use with Activity 6 on page 53.

6 **Ask and answer.** Ask your partner one question. Respond to your partner's question with the correct answer from the list below. Take turns.

Questions:

1. Will anyone watch the rocket launch on TV tomorrow?
2. Why don't aliens want to communicate with us?
3. Does everyone want people to travel in space?
4. Will someone in your family be an astronaut?

Answers for your partner:

a. Someone may want to go, but the trip takes many months.
b. We may all be able to see it if the sky is not cloudy.
c. Luis may know because he likes to study the solar system.
d. Someone can only breathe if the planet has an atmosphere like Earth's.

Unit 5 Student 2, use with Activity 3 on page 64.

3 **Ask and answer.** Respond to your partner's question with the correct answer from the right. Then ask your partner a question about a picture on the left.

a.

what kind / cloth / weave

1.

b.

what / family tradition / pass down

2.

Unit 7 Student 1, use with Activity 6 on page 93.

6 **Listen and answer.** Say the first half of a sentence from the first column. Your partner says the matching second half. Take turns. When you've said all the sentences, say three of your own!

Because of the book I read about volcanoes,

I know that some plants eat meat

She will visit a volcano this summer

If she completes her homework,

because he is tall and a good player.

if it snows too much.

I will play my favorite song.

I will get up early in the morning.

Unit 8 Student 1, use with Activity 3 on page 104.

3 **Ask and answer.** Ask your partner the question. When your partner asks you a question, respond with the correct answer. Take turns.

Questions:
Why should we conserve energy?
Why is it good to use natural materials?
How can we design better houses?
What can be done with chemicals?

Answers:
Plant a tree.
Keep paper out of the trash.
Sell or buy a used bicycle.
Turn off the computer at night.

5 **Work with a partner.** Read the instructions and play!

Heads
1 space

Tails
2 spaces

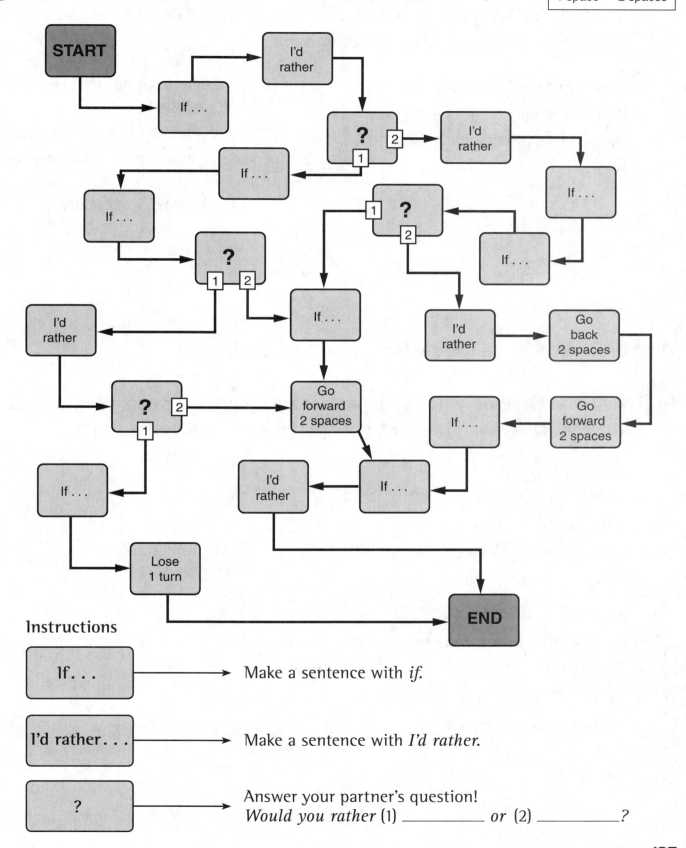

Instructions

| If . . . | → | Make a sentence with *if.* |

| I'd rather . . . | → | Make a sentence with *I'd rather.* |

| ? | → | Answer your partner's question!
Would you rather (1) _____ *or* (2) _____ ? |

Unit 7 Student 2, use with Activity 6 on page 93.

6 **Listen and answer.** Say the first half of a sentence from the first column. Your partner says the matching second half. Take turns. When you've said all the sentences, say three of your own!

Because of the fishing trip tomorrow,

If I learn to play the guitar,

He likes to play basketball

He will not go to school today

I know about eruptions that changed Earth's weather.

she will get a good grade on the test.

because of what I read about amazing plants.

if her family takes a vacation.

Unit 8 Student 2, use with Activity 3 on page 104.

3 **Ask and answer.** When your partner asks you a question, respond with the correct answer. Then ask your partner a question. Take turns.

Questions:

How can a bicycle be reused?

What can be done to recycle paper?

How can energy use be reduced?

How can the environment be renewed?

Answers:

Because it reduces the energy we need to make.

They should be made safe before being thrown away.

We can design them to conserve heat.

Because they are renewable.